AF771387

CONTENTS

WITNESSES

APPENDIX

REPORT CARD ON NAFTA

WEDNESDAY, MARCH 5, 1997

HOUSE OF REPRESENTATIVES,
SUBCOMMITTEE ON INTERNATIONAL ECONOMIC POLICY AND TRADE,
COMMITTEE ON INTERNATIONAL RELATIONS,
Washington, DC.

The Subcommittee met, pursuant to notice, at 2:07 p.m., room 2172, Rayburn House Office Building, Hon. Ileana Ros-Lehtinen, chair of the Subcommittee, presiding.

Ms. ROS-LEHTINEN. The Subcommittee will come to order.

The debate has been brewing in Washington over the last 3 years concerning the North American Free Trade Agreement (NAFTA) and it is indicative of a much larger debate taking place throughout our Nation. It underscores the need to address the concerns which have arisen about the impact of NAFTA on our U.S. economy before proceeding to further expand it.

In December 1994 at the Summit of the Americas held in my hometown of Miami, Florida, the three partners of NAFTA—the United States, Mexico and Canada—proceeded to extend an invitation to Chile to enter into the negotiations toward joining the free trade agreement. The Clinton Administration went on to express its view that Chile's inclusion in NAFTA would be a significant first step toward the creation of a Free Trade Area of the Americas by the year 2005—a goal that was established by the countries participating in the Miami summit.

Last week, as we know, the president of Chile visited Washington to discuss various issues which are key to the relations between his country and ours. At the top of his agenda, the potential accession of Chile into NAFTA and the outlook for "fast-track" authority to be granted by the U.S. Congress.

This, then, is a timely issue. It is a matter of importance to the American people, to the constituents that we, as Members of Congress, are here to serve. The pertinent U.S. Government agencies, some of whom are represented here today, are in the process of preparing an assessment of NAFTA's 3 years in effect, a report that was congressionally mandated. This Subcommittee will hold another hearing on NAFTA when that report is due.

However, if there are problems with NAFTA—if there is evidence to show that the reality is that it is not meeting the expectations set forth during the negotiations; if the problems are systemic or are procedural; if, in fact, there are no problems and the animosity toward NAFTA is simply due to lack of information or inaccurate data; then we must act and act now before it is too late to correct the situation.

In its ideal form, NAFTA was to open the borders of the three countries to liberalized trade which would stimulate economic growth in the three partner countries. It would open previously protected sectors in agriculture, energy, textiles and automotive trade. It was to open the U.S.-Mexico border to trade in services with specific guidelines in the field of financial services, transportation services and telecommunications. It was to lay the foundation for future North American economy based on high living standards, full employment and free and fair trade. It was set to improve working conditions and establish mechanisms to safeguard workers' rights in all three participant nations. Furthermore, its proponents argued that it would curtail illegal immigration into the United States from Mexico and would provide for a clean environment.

In essence, it was poised to be a miracle cure for many of the economic ills of the United States. However, as is usually the case with most "save all" cures, it was too good to be true. Serious deficiencies in the agreement have continued to afford Mexico an advantage over the United States by maintaining a low wage strategy, coupled with weak environmental, health and safety standards.

While some of the agreements have improved the original accord somewhat, the changes have not been sufficient to repair the endemic problems. As a result, the United States is recording trade deficits with most of its NAFTA partners, although as recently as the 1991 to 1994 period, the United States reported trade surpluses with Mexico.

There is evidence of flight of capital and labor, along with a redistribution of income within the U.S. economy which has been described as detrimental to the overall U.S. economic situation. Reports focusing on unemployment figures alone show the number of U.S. jobs lost due to NAFTA as of October, 1996, totaling 600,000.

This is but a sample of some of the issues that have been raised against NAFTA. Our witnesses in the second panel today have experienced firsthand numerous other problems which need immediate attention if we are to ensure that our citizens are not hurt by NAFTA.

In sum, the minimum requirements of NAFTA, and of any other trade agreement which our country enters into, is that it first does not harm. That is, even if the United States does not actually benefit from it, at least we should not suffer for it.

This is what we are here to determine today. Has the United States won or lost with NAFTA? For this purpose, we have invited a diverse group of witnesses who will provide their differing assessments of NAFTA's implementation and we thank them for being here with us today.

I would like to now recognize any other Member of our Subcommittee for any remark that they might have.

Thank you.

If not, we will first hear from the congressional panel and we are privileged to have Congressman Amo Houghton appearing before us, who will then be followed by Congressman Dave Bonior. Thank you both.

Amo.

Mr. HOUGHTON. Thank you very much, Madam Chairman. It is always a privilege and a pleasure to be with you. You have operated a wonderful Committee on Africa and I know you are doing a great job here.

I must say right off the bat that I am a big NAFTA supporter and so I want to show my true colors right away. I am not going to get into a numbers game. I have some testimony here which I would like to submit for the record.

Ms. ROS-LEHTINEN. Yes, we will be happy to accept the submission.

Mr. HOUGHTON. But I would like to talk about some general things.

The first thing is that there are some people that really do not like NAFTA—viscerally, biologically, chemically—they do not like it. And I have really great respect for some of my friends in the AFL/CIO and for Ross Perot and for Pat Choate and people like that and I understand where they are coming from. I just do not happen to agree with that. I think the only thing which I can do is to bring to the table a sort of a position of being a hardhat on trade because the company that I used to work for, because of the Japanese issue dumping of the products, virtually lost money for the first time in the early seventies in this century and that was because of dumped Japanese products into this country. So I understand the flight of capital and the flight of jobs and I hope I am sensitive to these conditions.

However, I did start a group, along with the IUD, which is the Industrial Union Department of the AFL/CIO, called Labor Industry Coalition on International Trade and I think we began to wrap our hands around issues, both from a management and a labor standpoint, which were helpful.

Let me just talk about several issues, the first is my district. I come from upstate New York and I know that there have been some problems. I know there was a company called Smith-Corona. It closed up its doors and went down to Mexico. I happen to think that most of the reason was for management purposes, for marketing purposes, not because of the flight of that company toward cheaper labor. But they did go to Mexico. And there are other examples where there are some problems.

However, on balance, I would like to feel that we have gained enormously from the trade with Mexico and, particularly, with the absence of the Maquilladoras. And that is, of course, what NAFTA fixed. I mean, there were not these little free trade unfair pockets which brought in products from the Far East and then with a small contributed value, moved those products into the United States almost as if it were another State. And I have taken trade groups down to Chile and to Argentina and we had a very successful one in Mexico and, as a result, the job creation from those and other records, I think has been on the plus side rather than the minus side. So what I am saying is, from the area I know best, which is in terms of products or geography, NAFTA has been a plus.

Let me just talk a little bit about the Maquilladoras. The Maquilladoras were these free trade areas I referred to earlier and they were really a problem. And they were a problem in an industry I know a little bit about, which is the television industry. The Japanese would bring products into the United States at a dump price. The dumping, ultimately and laboriously, was proved. The tariffs were raised. And what they did then is to divert the product to Mexico, add a small amount of contributed value, and brought it back into the United States through the Maquilladoras process. That is all out now. That was unfair and everybody agrees it was unfair.

So what has happened, really, since NAFTA on that particular product line is that the tariff has been increased here and so therefore the products coming from Japan cannot come in. They cannot come in any more from Mexico because of the absence of those little free trade Maquilladoras areas. So, really now, 90 percent of the large television—which is really what we consume, which is the 19-inch and larger—is made here in this country. For example, there is a little plant in State College making glass and they are increasing their production to the extent that they are putting $150 million into capital, another 1,000 jobs. That makes glass. The glass then goes to a little town called Horseheads, New York and Horseheads has a company called Toshiba. They make the tube. They are also adding the equivalent number of capital dollars and jobs.

Those products then—the glass and the tube—go down to Mexico and are made into a set. But 60 percent of the value of that set is in the tube. And then they come back into the United States. That never would have happened before. What would have happened is it would have come through the Maquilladoras directly from the Far East or, even before that, products would have come from the Far East.

Now you can say, “Well, that is only Japan because that has some sort of an order against it. What about Malaysia or Thailand or other countries like that?” Because of the economics of NAFTA, there is a 14-percent benefit in terms of manufactured products which now precludes all that from happening. So investment, job creation and all those things which happen to have hurt a company that I used to work for now are all changed. And I can give you other examples of that.

Let me just say a couple of other things. That I have always felt, since I was in business, that there was a competitor out there and we sometimes feel as if we are in this country that we can make a decision because there is no other country like it. We were a superpower. We can take our own mind. We can define the legislation any way we want. I do not happen to believe that. I think we are in competition with the diet. We are in competition with the Bundestag. We are not out there all by ourselves. And let me give you an example.

We went down to Chile—this is an all privately-sponsored trip—in November after the election and Chile is dabbling with the idea of joining the thing called Mercusur. Mercusur is a South American trading partnership. We do not have all the time in the world to decide on fast track with Chile because Chile would like our market and, obviously, the greatest asset we have is this precious mar-

REPORT CARD ON NAFTA

HEARING

BEFORE THE

SUBCOMMITTEE ON INTERNATIONAL ECONOMIC POLICY AND TRADE

OF THE

COMMITTEE ON INTERNATIONAL RELATIONS HOUSE OF REPRESENTATIVES

ONE HUNDRED FIFTH CONGRESS

FIRST SESSION

MARCH 5, 1997

Printed for the use of the Committee on International Relations

U.S. GOVERNMENT PRINTING OFFICE

44–878 CC WASHINGTON : 1998

For sale by the U.S. Government Printing Office
Superintendent of Documents, Congressional Sales Office, Washington, DC 20402
ISBN 0-16-056023-3

COMMITTEE ON INTERNATIONAL RELATIONS

BENJAMIN A. GILMAN, New York, *Chairman*

WILLIAM GOODLING, Pennsylvania
JAMES A. LEACH, Iowa
HENRY J. HYDE, Illinois
DOUG BEREUTER, Nebraska
CHRISTOPHER SMITH, New Jersey
DAN BURTON, Indiana
ELTON GALLEGLY, California
ILEANA ROS-LEHTINEN, Florida
CASS BALLENGER, North Carolina
DANA ROHRABACHER, California
DONALD A. MANZULLO, Illinois
EDWARD R. ROYCE, California
PETER T. KING, New York
JAY KIM, California
STEVEN J. CHABOT, Ohio
MARSHALL "MARK" SANFORD, South Carolina
MATT SALMON, Arizona
AMO HOUGHTON, New York
TOM CAMPBELL, California
JON FOX, Pennsylvania
JOHN McHUGH, New York
LINDSEY GRAHAM, South Carolina
ROY BLUNT, Missouri
JERRY MORAN, Kansas
KEVIN BRADY, Texas

LEE HAMILTON, Indiana
SAM GEJDENSON, Connecticut
TOM LANTOS, California
HOWARD BERMAN, California
GARY ACKERMAN, New York
ENI F.H. FALEOMAVAEGA, American Samoa
MATTHEW G. MARTINEZ, California
DONALD M. PAYNE, New Jersey
ROBERT ANDREWS, New Jersey
ROBERT MENENDEZ, New Jersey
SHERROD BROWN, Ohio
CYNTHIA A. McKINNEY, Georgia
ALCEE L. HASTINGS, Florida
PAT DANNER, Missouri
EARL HILLIARD, Alabama
WALTER CAPPS, California
BRAD SHERMAN, California
ROBERT WEXLER, Florida
DENNIS J. KUCINICH, Ohio
STEVE ROTHMAN, New Jersey
BOB CLEMENT, Tennessee
BILL LUTHER, Minnesota
JIM DAVIS, Florida

RICHARD J. GARON, *Chief of Staff*
MICHAEL H. VAN DUSEN, *Democratic Chief of Staff*

SUBCOMMITTEE ON INTERNATIONAL ECONOMIC POLICY AND TRADE

ILEANA ROS-LEHTINEN, Florida, *Chairperson*

DONALD A. MANZULLO, Illinois
STEVEN J. CHABOT, Ohio
TOM CAMPBELL, California
LINDSEY O. GRAHAM, South Carolina
ROY BLUNT, Missouri
JERRY MORAN, Kansas
KEVIN BRADY, Texas
DOUG BEREUTER, Nebraska
DANA ROHRABACHER, California

SAM GEJDENSON, Connecticut
PAT DANNER, Missouri
EARL F. HILLIARD, Alabama
BRAD SHERMAN, California
STEVEN R. ROTHMAN, New Jersey
BOB CLEMENT, Tennessee
TOM LANTOS, California
BILL LUTHER, Minnesota

MAURICIO TAMARGO, *Chief of Staff*
YLEEM D.S. POBLETE, *Professional Staff Member*
AMOS HOCHSTEIN, *Democratic Professional Staff Member*
JOSE A. FUENTES, *Staff Associate*

ket. But, at the same time, they do not need it. They can go to Argentina. They can go to Brazil. They can go to other places. So timing is very important and we must make a decision whether we want to continue these regional relationships such as we have with Mexico and Canada to Chile and Argentina and other people like that who want to be part of our team here.

Another thing I think is important—and this is really my last point—is that you must look at a trading agreement in the long term. That is what it really has been geared for. We have had the collapse of the peso, the numbers have been swamped by that very unusual monetary adjustment. We cannot rely on them. NAFTA really is not going to be scheduled to be fully effective until January of the year 2000. And also, if you take a look at some of the statements which come out of the White House about the ten million new jobs which have been created in the last 4 years, some of that has got to come from NAFTA-related areas.

So I believe that this is a good treaty. I believe that we ought to really think of ourselves as part of a world in which 95 percent of the customers for this country are outside the United States. And we must do those things which will consolidate our base and I think NAFTA is one of them.

Thank you very much.

[The prepared statement of Mr. Houghton appears in the appendix.]

Ms. ROS-LEHTINEN. Thank you so much, Amo. We appreciate it.

We are honored to also have with us Mr. Bonior from Michigan, who is the House Democratic Whip. Thank you, Dave.

Mr. BONIOR. Thank you, Madam Chairperson. I appreciate your having this hearing. I want to commend you for that and for your tireless commitment on this issue. I also want to say how honored I am to be with my friend and colleague, Mr. Houghton, who is one of the most serious and well thought of Members in this body and who, when he speaks, I certainly listen. And while we may have a disagreement on this issue, I value his judgment and his thinking in this institution very much.

I want to thank you for giving me the opportunity to appear here today. Four years ago this country had a very major debate over NAFTA and those of us who fought for a better treaty back then—one that protects labor rights and human rights and the environment—are just as determined to make sure that the faults of NAFTA are addressed today.

This debate is moving into a new phase. Supporters of the NAFTA agreement now want to expand NAFTA into new countries. But expanding NAFTA now would be like building a new room onto your house when your kitchen is on fire and your roof is collapsing. Before we expand NAFTA, we have to fix it. And, believe me, there is a lot to fix.

This is no longer a question of theory. NAFTA has had 38 months to prove itself. Most of us have waited patiently. We have not loaded our guns during that 38-month period and shot our fire at the treaty. We wanted to see if it would work. We hoped that it would work. But we have seen the effects that NAFTA has had on our families and our jobs and on our country. And it is not good news.

I believe that NAFTA has been, for the most part, another failure. Our trade deficit with Mexico is now a record $16 billion and I know the peso has something to do with it, but let me just tell my friends who are into that argument that even before the collapse of the peso, 5 or 6 months prior to that collapse, the deficit was increasing with Mexico. So it is not just the peso.

And, by the way, on the peso issue, we argued vehemently—those of us who opposed NAFTA 38 months ago—that, in fact, that was one of the deficiencies, that it did not consider the value of the peso in the discussion of NAFTA and it certainly should have been a very important part of any agreement.

Using a very narrow definition by the Department of Labor, more than 100,000 Americans have lost their jobs to NAFTA. And using the proponents' own formula, as the Chairperson mentioned in her opening statement, about 600,000 Americans have lost their jobs. Now, these trends were in place long before, as I said, the peso devaluation.

If the peso devaluation were the only reason, other nations would suffer trade deficits as well. But Japan and other European nations have maintained their surpluses before, during and after the peso crash. It is primarily the agreement, not the peso, which is causing our deficit. Ninety percent of the companies who promise to create jobs have not. Sixty-five percent of the workers who were laid off ended up with lower paying jobs. Fifty-seven percent of Americans now say their purchasing power is worse than it was before NAFTA. And, most importantly, and I want to emphasize this, the Labor Department found that 62 percent of companies are now using Mexico and other low-wage nations as bargaining chips to drive down wages. It is happening all over the country.

In Mexico, the situation is even worse. The Mexican economy, as a whole, has collapsed. Along the border, production has soared but wages have fallen by 25 percent. Workers in the Maquilladoras no longer make a dollar an hour. They now make 70 cents an hour. And workers who try to form unions are still being fired and thrown into jail.

Madam Chairperson, I was just there a few weeks ago. I went down to the Maquilladoras outside of Tijuana and I can tell you things are not better. They are worse. They are worse from a wage standpoint. They are worse from these workers—wonderful workers, wonderful people trying to make a living for their families—being arrested when they try to shut a line down that is causing bodily injury to their relatives' hands and fingers. People protesting and then being arrested, then being fired.

The situation is not good. It is not good from an environmental standpoint and I could spend a good hour with you on that, but I know we do not have the time. But I would love to get into the discussion about the environmental degradation that continues along our border.

NAFTA has not created a consumer market in Mexico. It has created an export platform. As a Nation, we now ship more consumer goods to Switzerland than we do to Mexico. A good example is the auto industry. From 1994 to 1995, production in the Maquilladoras for the domestic Mexican market plummeted by 72 percent. The production for export to the United States grew by 36 percent. We are selling fewer cars in Mexico and shipping more back here and, as a result, our trade deficit in the auto sector ballooned to more than $15 billion.

Meanwhile, the environment is suffering the consequences. Families along the border continue to live near, bathe in and drink the water that American Medical Association has called—and I quote—"a cesspool of infectious disease." This is the AMA.

The North American Development Bank, which was set up to fix these problems, we all remember that debate. That was going to solve some of the environmental problems on the border. But after 38 months, the bank has yet to make a single meaningful loan for the public good. And, what is more, NAFTA has helped create what some called a waveline border check. Eleven thousand trucks now pass over the border from Mexico every day and for every truck that gets inspected, 199 do not. They are just waved through and God knows what is on them. Every single week seems to bring another story of corruption at the highest levels of the Mexican Government.

Is this tragic? Of course it is. Is it permanent? No. We still believe that NAFTA can be a force for progress. We always believed that. We still believe that it can create a consumer market in Mexico. But before we even think about expanding NAFTA to other countries, we need to fix the flaws in it. We need to give workers the same kind of labor and health protections that we gave companies for things like intellectual property. We need to include labor and environmental standards in the core agreement, not in any side agreements. We need to raise Mexico's standards to our level and not lower ours to theirs. And we need to make non-compliance subject to sanctions, not just consultations.

We need to remember this is not just about markets and trade barriers. This is about jobs and living standards. It is about human rights and it is about human dignity. Workers on both sides of the border are mistreated by multinational corporations and indifferent government. But they remain brave and they remain hopeful. Until they have a voice to fight for themselves, we must continue to be their voice, Madam Chairman.

There are more people in this Congress who voted against NAFTA 4 years ago than voted for it. And the many who voted for it say they would never vote for it again. Before we expand NAFTA, we have got to fix what does not work. We believe we can. We are going to work hard in the months ahead to do just that.

And if I could just end with this note—my friend from New York State mentioned the television industry and I had the chance to go to a community, colonia, near the Panasonic plant and the Samsung plant and I want to tell you that while they are producing these television sets for export into this country primarily, the workers who are making those sets are working for $5 and $6 a day and then they go back to homes which I visited in colonia that are disparate in their construction, often without running water, without sanitation facilities and, of course, next to facilities and factories and shops that spew chemicals and poisons into their rivers and streams in which they bathe and take water. It is a really sad situation and I think it is incumbent upon us to do all that we can to fix this NAFTA before we go on and offer it to other countries.

I thank the gentlelady.

Ms. ROS-LEHTINEN. Thank you so much, Mr. Bonior.

Mr. Gejdenson, the Ranking Member, could not be with us today because of a long-scheduled conflict. However, we will be entering his remarks into the record as well as any other Member who would like to enter them.

[At press time the statement had not been submitted.]

Ms. ROS-LEHTINEN. And, based on a previous agreement between Sam and me, we decided that because of the number of witnesses and the time restraints we will only have one question from each side following the congressional testimony. On our side we will have Mr. Brady and Ms. Danner on the Democrat side.

Mr. Brady.

Mr. BRADY. Thank you, Madam Chairman.

I am a Member from Texas and from the Houston region and, obviously, our State is a thermometer for the NAFTA agreement, both in trucking issues and environmental issues and in the immigration problems that occur because there is not a strong economy on the Mexican side. And, without question, the trade agreement is not perfect. But wouldn't you agree—and either of the witnesses feel free to reply—that this is a long-term issue? That the goal here is to create a predictable set of rules that allow business to invest in both countries that allow them the type of consistency to create jobs?

I have noticed that within our sectors, institutions that create jobs support NAFTA. Those who accept jobs often have problems with them. And since the goal here is to strengthen the economy of all the countries involved, I guess the bottom line is isn't it extremely premature to make any assessment of NAFTA at this time? I mean, it is not fully implemented. We are creating a trade vehicle. We have barely put the chassis together and have not seen yet how it performs long-term. Wouldn't you agree that it is premature to be making significant decisions when we have not yet seen the results?

Mr. HOUGHTON. Would you like me to answer, or Mr. Bonior?

Mr. BRADY. Yes, please. Yes, sir.

Mr. HOUGHTON. Well, I agree with you. I mean, clearly, we do not want to have our country end up as a warehouse for products we cannot afford to buy and that is a given. But you have to remember that there is really a very close allegiance of the Mexican people to the Americans. As an example, $7 out of $10 of imported products comes from this country. They want to buy from us. They want to be friends with us. And I know that the environmental laws are not perfect, and I know the labor laws are not perfect, and I know they should have more health care, and I know there should be better pensions, and I know there should be better eating standards and the whole thing like that. They are working up on this and the perfect example is to go to a place like Monterey. Monterey and, obviously, Mexico City, are the two key areas, Monterey being the industrial base. And it is moving and it is changing.

But I think that when you take a look at a program like this, you cannot look at it in only a few months and I agree with you.

It has to be over a longer term and that is what the whole concept of NAFTA was.

Mr. BRADY. Thank you, sir.

Mr. BONIOR. We have had 38 months to look at this and if we are going to take the position that there is no need to correct any of this, then we are in for a horrendous, horrendous experience in the next couple of years. I would just commend to you a book that William Greyer just wrote, "One World, Ready or Not: the Manic Logic of Global Capitalism." And we in this country can only for so long continue to be the purchaser of surplus goods from places like Mexico and China. And it is catching up with us. It is catching up with us in the loss of good wage jobs. It is catching up with us in terms of the huge trade deficits that we are piling up that are reaching alarming proportions.

Long-term? Yes, we should look at it from a long-term perspective. But the missing piece, I think, in your statement, sir, was setting up rules for business. What about setting up rules for workers? What about setting up rules for the vast majority of people who have to suffer in a situation in which they cannot organize, they cannot assemble, they are restricted in their free speech, they are thrown in jail if they attempt to do so.

And, with all due respect, we are going backwards over there. We are going backwards in many respects on labor and environmental standards. We are not moving forward. And so I think that both of those pieces—the environmental piece as well as the labor piece—need to be a part of any future agreement and any corrections in order for the Mexican workers to harmonize up on standards and health with what we have here in the United States.

Mr. BRADY. Thank you, Ma'am.

Ms. ROS-LEHTINEN. Thank you so much, Mr. Brady.

Ms. Danner.

Ms. DANNER. Thank you, Madam Chairman.

I respect both my colleagues. Obviously, they have differing opinions and I fall on the side of Congressman Bonior. And my question to you, Amo, will ultimately be how long do you think that it should take because you said we have not had a long enough period of time, but we have had over 3 years.

Let me just say that 2 weeks ago over 300 people in my district learned that their jobs were going to Mexico. They manufacture shoes. And in talking with my staffers about it, I learned that we will have immediate help from the Department of Labor because any employee in shoe manufacturing, is assumed if they are displaced by someone in Mexico, immediate help is available. We do not have to go through the general loops and hoops that we have to go through in most instances. In effect, it seems to me as though the Department of Labor has said, "If you are manufacturing shoes in America, you may lose your job to Mexico. But we are going to help you just right away without a lot of preamble to it." That is very sad.

Just prior to that, several months ago, Lee Jeans, also in my district, announced that they were moving their manufacturing operations of over 400 jobs to Mexico. I personally spoke with the chairman of the company that owns Lee Jeans, Vanity Fair, and he told me that they were almost forced to go to Mexico. That they were forced to leave the country because their competitors were doing it and if they were going to remain competitive, they had to leave the country also.

I have had others leave the country. Sherwood Medical. They did not really tell us where they were moving their equipment. We only know they moved it out of the United States, so we are told. I cannot find any evidence at all of anything that has been a plus for my congressional district in NAFTA and I am very concerned about it.

Rather like David, I, too, have had an opportunity to go to Mexico and I am sure that you probably have, too. I saw the people who manufacture televisions down there. One gentleman who was wearing very proudly his Zenith T-shirt. But he is never going to have an opportunity to watch television because he does not have any electricity in the home he showed us. He showed us his home very proudly. They literally sweep the dirt out of their home because they are living on dirt. And when it is raining, they live on mud and in mud. It was just beyond belief.

We saw people who work and live in these colonias who were drinking water from streams that had dead animals in them. I mean, the human rights violations down there, I could go on and on about different stories that we were told as we visited the different colonias and talked with the different people. It is very difficult for an American worker to compete with someone who will work for cents per hour and who will work with no safeguards whatsoever.

I believe that over 3 years, it seems to me, to be adequate and I will not even get into the issue that I feel very strongly about being a Member of transportation with regard to the trucks. But my question is, how long do you think we should take to look at this issue and rectify some of the problems that exist?

Mr. HOUGHTON. Well, Ms. Danner, I do not know. How big is a pile of stones? You just do not really know. I think that the authors of NAFTA recognized that it was going to be a multi-year process, at best. And, as I said earlier in my testimony, that this thing really is not supposed to kick in full speed until January of the year 2000.

Now, all the problems will not be solved by that time and there are going to continue to be problems. But there are problems such as you described in Mexico and Malaysia and Thailand and Indonesia and places like that and we should be concerned with jobs. There is not any question about it. But I think that some of the companies that I have seen operate have been able to translate their technology as they move out of low technical areas—and this does not necessarily help the shoe or the fabric industry—but they have been able to supplement jobs in the high-tech area.

For example, there have been some consumer products in our area that have moved outside the United States. Not to Mexico but to other places. Where, at the same time, there have been two or three major expansions in terms of optical fiber in our area. Those jobs happen to pay three times what the other jobs did, despite the fact they are both unionized, because of the high technical content of this thing. So I think it is going to be a long time, but we just have to understand that these countries are trying to pull themselves up by their bootstraps.

And you may be right in terms of rats running around and dirt floors and things like that. I have not seen that in the plants with which I have been associated in Mexico. And now, granted, they are particularly around the metropolitan areas such as Mexico City and Monterey. These people who live in, probably not the type of house that you or I would live in, but reasonable housing. They do not have dirt floors. They buy a lot of American products. They walk around in American-style clothes. Those are the people, obviously, that are going to make the difference in the economy uptick in Mexico.

Ms. ROS-LEHTINEN. Thank you so much. Thank you.

I know Congressman Houghton is needed in another Subcommittee so we are going to excuse him.

Mr. Bonior, if it is possible, Mr. Sherman just has a quick question.

Mr. BONIOR. Sure.

Ms. ROS-LEHTINEN. If it is possible for you to stick around for a few minutes.

Mr. BONIOR. Yes.

Ms. ROS-LEHTINEN. Thank you so much, Amo.

Mr. HOUGHTON. Thank you very much.

Mr. SHERMAN. When we have a completely open market, NAFTA-designed, with another country, naturally when there is an American factory, that factory has to compete with the concept of moving those jobs to another location where there may be different wages and different environmental standards. And it makes some sense for us to perhaps have free trade agreements with countries that have democratic institutions so that the people there will insist upon high environmental standards and other countries that protect worker rights so that they are going to have wages coming up to our level.

David, I wonder, when you think in terms of democratic institutions, environmental protection and worker rights, whether countries like Australia and Sweden come to mind, or do you think in terms of Chile and Brazil as being good partners?

Mr. BONIOR. Well——

Mr. SHERMAN. It is a rhetorical question.

Mr. BONIOR. It is. And Chile has made some progress, I think we have to recognize that, in terms of democracy but I take your point.

What we are saying, and we are trying to get the Administration and our colleagues who are on the other side of this issue to focus in on, is that there has to be at least a minimum standard in the environment and on worker rights and on human rights.

You know, when the Europeans did the European Union, entry into that was conditioned upon countries meeting a certain standard. They did not allow Spain and Greece into the European Union, and Turkey, until they met a certain standard and those countries agreed with it and they worked toward that standard and they actually got some support from the other European countries to meet that standard and then they worked out the problems. What we are doing here is quite unprecedented and, in fact, is lowering our standards or certainly our workers' standards and wages in this country to a situation which we are finding a widening income gap between those who have and those who have not in America. And it is very, very dangerous.

And so, just to conclude, I would suggest that what we are offering here is an opportunity for workers on both sides of the border to win. Right now, workers on both sides of the borders are losing. The corporations.

And I might just add, parenthetically here, that these multinational corporations, some of them with great names that we have been familiar with all of our lives, have really no shame. No shame in what they are doing down on the border in the Maquilladoras area. Some of them even from my home area.

They go down there, they pay these pathetic wages. They provide very little opportunity for these people in a variety of different ways. And these are modern facilities.

Amo talked about seeing these factories and these facilities and the people working as being clean and modern. They are clean and modern, for the most part, in the Maquilladoras areas and many of them are. They are state-of-the-art. And the workers, the Mexican workers, are very good workers. But they are not getting rewarded for what they are doing and, of course, they cannot afford the product that they are producing, as Pat Danner just indicated.

So until we deal with the basic ability for them to organize and collectively bargain for a decent wage, as our workers struggled to do at the early part of this century, we are not going to see the democratization process in the workplace or in the political sector that is necessary for us to have an equal partnership similar to what we have with Canada.

Thank you.

Ms. ROS-LEHTINEN. Thank you so much, David. We appreciate you being here today with us.

As our next panel gets settled, I would like to proceed with their introductions. Leading the discussion will be Ambassador Ira Shapiro, who serves as senior counsel and negotiator in the Office of the U.S. Trade Representative. Previously, he has served as the USTR's general counsel playing a major role in the negotiation of the NAFTA side agreement and the completion of the Uruguay Round. Ambassador Shapiro served in the government prior to his tenure at USTR when he worked as Minority staff director and chief counsel to the Governmental Affairs Committee, counsel for the Senate Majority leader and chief of staff, Senator John D. Rockefeller.

He will be followed by Regina Vargo, who serves as Deputy Assistant Secretary of Commerce for the Western Hemisphere. She is responsible within the Department for the implementation of the U.S.-Canada Free Trade Agreement and prior to this position, she served as the director of the Office of NAFTA. During this tenure, she earned two gold medals, the Department's highest award, for her contribution to the NAFTA negotiations and for her role in developing the Export Mexico Program.

We thank them both for being here today and we will begin with Ambassador Shapiro.

STATEMENT OF AMBASSADOR IRA SHAPIRO, SENIOR COUNSEL AND NEGOTIATOR, OFFICE OF THE U.S. TRADE REPRESENTATIVE

Mr. SHAPIRO. Thank you, Madam Chairman, for the opportunity to appear here today to discuss the NAFTA. I think that an inquiry on NAFTA after 3 years is certainly well worthwhile and the first panel and some of the comments remind me that there are very few subjects still that are as controversial as the NAFTA. You often feel like you are talking about not only two different views of a trade agreement but two different views of our economy and related issues. And David Bonior, particularly, and Ms. Danner have raised so many issues that there will be some danger in being able to confront them all effectively.

But, since personal notes usually get introduced here, let me just offer one personal note. I spent most of the 1980's trying to think about what a democratic trade policy would look like if the Democrats ever got into power. I thought that our trade policy, and a lot of us thought that our trade policy, in the seventies and eighties was not working. That we were involved in one-way trade so that we were an open market and the other markets were closed to us. It was a carryover from the 1950's and 1960's when our prosperity was something we could take for granted. And a lot of us—and that includes a lot of my friends in the Congress, the AFL/CIO, the UAW—thought quite a bit about what a trade policy might look like or what it would take to restore U.S. competitiveness if we ever got the chance to do it. And, frankly, I would argue that we have done a pretty good job in the last 4 years and that we have had a fair amount of unity in doing it, with the exception of NAFTA.

NAFTA is the one issue that still divides people who are absolutely committed to a strong U.S. economy and a strong trade policy. But we come down on two different sides. So I would like to start, having stated that background, in looking for a little common ground here which often does not exist on NAFTA.

And let me say first, Congressman Bonior put forth a number of issues and I would just like to state a few questions to hang out there as we talk about this. The first is, I think, whether Congressman Bonior and others' description of where our economy is now is accurate. Is it accurate to talk about this job loss? Is he reflecting the economy that you understand to be in our country today? My answer, by the way, will be no.

The second is an overriding question—whether we would somehow be better off without NAFTA. I would ask whether we would be better off without NAFTA or whether Mexico would be better off without NAFTA. And I think I am going to answer that, or at least suggest that the answer is negative there, too.

The third question, though, is—because he talks about changing NAFTA, a different NAFTA—the third question is whether the NAFTA that he is seeking is attainable. Whether it is possible somehow to have a trade agreement in which we specify labor standards, environmental standards, pensions, the sort that he is describing. And I do not think, for a variety of reasons, that is realistic, but it is a difficult subject to get through.

And the last, I suppose, since we have heard concerns about the Mexican people, is whether they would somehow be better off without NAFTA. And I think, basically, the answer to that is no as well.

Let me start by saying that NAFTA——

Ms. ROS-LEHTINEN. It worries me when the yellow light comes on and you start that phrase saying, "Let me start—".

Mr. SHAPIRO. Well——

Ms. ROS-LEHTINEN. That is a problem.

Mr. SHAPIRO. Congresswoman, I suppose I should have asked how much time I really have. Five more? Or five total?

NAFTA has been a key component of our trade policy. It was not a favor we did Mexico. When we looked at trade when we came into office, we found the terms of trade with Mexico were not right. That the Mexican market was too closed to our products. And that the barriers to all kinds of U.S. products were too high. When we passed NAFTA and when Congress implemented NAFTA, most of the changes, the overwhelming number of changes, were required of Mexico because they had to change their trade regime and we did not change ours.

Now, the second thing, since I am conscious of what the Chairwoman said, is this question of our economy today. It seems our destiny to debate not only NAFTA, but the condition of our economy. Today our economy is the envy of much of the world because of its job creation rate and its low inflation rate and its strength across the board. We set the pace in diverse fields. Our industrial production has been up 18 percent in 4 years and we have expanded industrial capacity to the highest level since the 1970's. We have come back in sectors that were in deep trouble 5 and 10 years ago—autos and auto parts, steel and semiconductors, machine tools. Our performance has been quite strong in much of the Nation.

But, if you look at certain parts of the industrial midwest, there has been a particularly strong renaissance and I wish Congress Bonior was here because I do not intend to bring these points up in his absence, but Michigan, of all the States in the Nation, Michigan has the fastest rate of income growth for the last 4 years. Michigan's unemployment, I think, is at 4.9 percent. The income growth rate is 5.8 percent and there has been a significant pocket in which there has actually been shortage of skilled workers.

Now, throughout the upper midwest, there has been a renaissance on in terms of production and in terms of manufacturing and exports have played a crucial part in that resurgence. I appeared with Governor Jim Edgar of Illinois in Chicago last year and he stated that NAFTA was working for the benefit of Illinois workers and their families. In the first——

Ms. ROS-LEHTINEN. If you could summarize your statement now. Thank you, Ambassador.

Mr. SHAPIRO. I will try. I am sorry.

Three things I will say quickly, or relatively quickly. The first is, NAFTA proved to be a buffer against a loss of exports for us when the peso prices hit. The Mexican economy came back much more rapidly. Mexico did not close their market to our exports. They went on with their NAFTA commitments.

In the 1980's, we lost 50 percent of our exports when they had a financial problem. This time, we lost 9 percent and snapped back in 18 months.

The second thing I would simply say—and I would obviously like to get into more in length—the labor and environmental side agreements that we insisted on as part of the NAFTA have started to have positive effects. By no means have they transformed the situation in Mexico as yet. But the labor side agreement has brought important freedom of association issues to the fore in Mexico and they continue to be the serious subject of debate there. For instance, the Mexican Supreme Court found recently that State laws restricting union organization in State government is unconstitutional. And in my written statement, I would like to submit a list of examples——

Ms. ROS-LEHTINEN. Thank you. We will be glad to enter your statement into the record.

Thank you so much, Ambassador. We appreciate you being here with us.

Ms. Vargo.

STATEMENT OF REGINA K. VARGO, DEPUTY ASSISTANT SECRETARY FOR THE WESTERN HEMISPHERE, DEPARTMENT OF COMMERCE

Ms. VARGO. Thank you very much, Madam Chairman, for the opportunity to appear here today. I do have a longer statement I would like to submit for the record and will try to summarize a few key points here.

The U.S.-NAFTA trade relationship is the largest one that the United States has in the world. Our NAFTA partners both buy and sell $3 out of every $10 that the United States exports and imports. Almost one third of the current trade levels that are taking place between the United States and NAFTA is new trade that has taken place since we implemented NAFTA 3 years ago. We think NAFTA has met its objectives of expanding and protecting U.S. exports to Mexico and Canada.

While NAFTA phases out tariff barriers over 15 years, most of the trade that is taking place within NAFTA is already duty-free. Next January, the last tariffs between the United States and Canada will be eliminated. Mexican tariffs, which had averaged about 10 percent prior to NAFTA, will now average less than 6 percent, with tough rules of origin that reward companies for using North American parts and labor, an incentive that increases as these duties are phased out.

Tariff barriers are only one impediment that has kept U.S. companies from market access. Just as significant can be non-tariff barriers. That has certainly been the case with the Mexican auto regime. In 1993, we estimated that removing Mexico's auto restrictions would open up $1 billion in new export opportunities for U.S. auto companies, and it has. In 1996, the United States exported 51,000 new passenger cars and 31,500 new trucks to Mexico valued at $1.2 billion, despite the situation within the Mexican economy.

As Ambassador Shapiro has suggested, in contrast to the 1982 Mexican economic crisis, U.S. exports to Mexico fell by only 9 percent in the year following the 1994 peso devaluation, despite a drop in the Mexican economy of 7 percent. This is the case because NAFTA locked in Mexico's trade opening and its economic reforms. NAFTA helped the Mexican economy get back to a much quicker and stronger recovery than most forecasters predicted with the return of Mexican economic growth of 5.1 percent last year—a very impressive record from the debt they were in. Our exports reached a record $57 billion and their growth is accelerating. If these trends continue, the trade deficit will narrow this year and our market share will grow.

Responding to further privatizations and new opportunities, U.S. exports of capital goods increased 17 percent last year. U.S. exports of industrial goods rose 21 percent. And the Zedillo Administration is forecasting economic growth of 4 percent next year for the Mexican economy with the interesting point being, I think, that half of this growth is seen as coming from a pickup in domestic consumption in Mexico as employment levels and real wages begin to rise.

U.S. imports from Mexico also set a new record in 1996. Mexico's exports enabled it to weather the economic crisis and pay back 3 years early its debt to the United States. Some of these imports are substituting for imports from other sources and some relate to coproduction agreements which strengthen U.S. competitiveness. Both of these are issues that we will be examining in the larger NAFTA study due to Congress on July 1 of this year.

In discussing NAFTA, it is also important to remember that the U.S.-Canada relationship is the largest in the world. Unfortunately, last year the Canadian economy was marked by relatively low growth and a high unemployment rate and a falling Canadian dollar depressed demand for U.S. products, which nonetheless still managed to reach $134 billion. Like Mexico, Canadian economic growth will pick up this year.

Now, there is a lot of discussion about winners or losers within NAFTA. But I think it is interesting to note that about half of U.S. trade in both directions, with Mexico and with Canada, takes place in just three industries—motor vehicles and parts, industrial machinery and computers, and electric and electronic equipment—and that regionalization under NAFTA appears to be intensifying local specializations within industries, rather than discretely allocating industries among countries.

Finally, recognizing the benefits of freer trade, many countries in Latin America have formed regional trading agreements, such as Mercusur, that have seen significant increases in internal trade as their barriers come down, just as we have seen in NAFTA. But we are not members of those agreements, setting our exporters at a competitive disadvantage. And to cite just one example, Southwest Bell recently chose to source from Northern Telecomm in Canada $180 million in telecommunications equipment for a project in Chile, rather than from U.S. suppliers, because it would save them nearly $20 million in tariffs, thanks to the Free Trade Agreement that Canada has negotiated with Chile.

Madam Chairman, we need to address these competitive disadvantages and create a Free Trade Area of the Americas based on principles that put our firms and farms on equal footing with their hemispheric competition.

In closing, I would just like to say at the Commerce Department we have been very active in providing information on these new opportunities for U.S. exporters and smaller firms and there is a tremendous amount of interest out there for that. I might just note one point. Last year, we provided over 74,000 documents alone discussing what the market opportunities in Mexico were.

I think the record shows that NAFTA works for U.S., Mexican and Canadian firms and workers. It opens new market opportunities. It helps enhance our competitiveness in the markets of our NAFTA partners, in our domestic market, and in overseas markets. And it has aided the Mexican recovery.

Thank you and I would be happy to answer any questions.

[The prepared statement of Ms. Vargo appears in the appendix.]

Ms. ROS-LEHTINEN. Thank you. Thank you so much, both of our panelists.

We have been joined by Congresswoman Marcy Kaptur, who, due to a schedule conflict, could not be here with the earlier panel. But we are honored that she has joined us now.

Marcy, thank you.

Ms. KAPTUR. Thank you, Madam Chairwoman and Members of the Committee. It is a pleasure to be with you today, especially on a subject near and dear to the hearts of the constituents that I represent and I want to commend you for your interest in helping prepare a report card on NAFTA. If it is truly to be a blueprint for the hemisphere then now, over 3 years since its passage, it probably makes a great deal of sense for us to be very objective in our measurement of its results.

Let me say that, in my own view, NAFTA is causing serious structural damage inside this economy and it is also creating instability in North America as a whole. Some corporations have benefited in both nations from this situation. However, in the aggregate, I believe NAFTA has really worked to, unfortunately, provide a tarnished blueprint for the hemisphere. And my own perspective today would be for us to go back to renegotiate certain provisions of NAFTA to make them work before we then extend it to include other nations. And I would like to discuss that a bit.

A bill that I introduced today, along with over three dozen colleagues on a bipartisan basis, the NAFTA Accountability Act of 1997, builds on the momentum we developed in the last 104th Congress when we obtained over 110 co-sponsors over a 2-year period. We now have over three dozen on the first day of introduction. So I think that there is a growing consensus within the Congress, within our membership, that there are parts of NAFTA that are definitely not working and, with the help of committees such as your own, we can right the situation.

Let me review some of the provisions of our bill. We asked the Administration, the executive branch, to actually measure against certain performance standards how NAFTA has actually worked. And if NAFTA lives up to those standards, terrific. If it does not, then we ask the Administration to renegotiate in the following areas:

One concerns the trade deficit—the account balance with the nations of Canada and Mexico. It takes a look at the job situation for our people as well as the other countries. It takes a look at environment. Human rights and democracy, immigration, the whole question of truck standards and truck safety and also illicit drug trade. And we ask for certification in these areas. In addition, there are agricultural provisions in our measure and currency provisions because of the difficulties——

We had tried to get courtesy provisions in the original NAFTA bill. They were not allowed in by the Committee and then we were faced with the peso devaluation. So we have provisions in the NAFTA Accountability Act that deal with that.

I wanted to say a word about some of these. The testimony covers them in full. But let me talk about the trade deficit.

Now, is there an overall chart there for the overall U.S. merchandise trade—OK.

If you look at this chart, that gives you a sense of what has been happening to the United States over the last 25 years in terms of our overall trade accounts. You will see that the trade deficits this country has been amassing are growing larger and larger as the share of GDP, in real terms and nominal terms. And they are coming in waves and they are getting deeper.

If one were to estimate, taking the $150, $160-billion dollar trade deficit from last year and the NAFTA account, our deficits with Canada and Mexico, are $40 billion of that $160 billion—25 percent and growing. That cuts off, shaves, 1 percent off GDP in any year. So if we grow at a weak 2.5 or 2.7 percent, 2.8 percent—we are creating jobs and temporary work with no benefits, restaurant jobs, health care jobs, the three major job growth areas over the last 5 years—what you are doing is, you are trading off good jobs with good wages and benefits for the substitutional jobs in our marketplace and the fact that wages are not rising and benefits are not rising means that we are actually having a pulldown in our own standard of living across this country. The significance of this 1 percent off a low GDP growth rate is extremely significant to the people of this country.

Now, we were told that NAFTA would give us a trade surplus in the first year. It has not only not given us a trade surplus, it has given us the worst historic deficit with both Mexico and Canada that we have ever had. Each billion dollars of trade, the Administration agrees, translates into about 20,000 jobs. So when you think about a $40-billion trade deficit with Canada and Mexico last year, you are beginning to talk real jobs. If you look at the number of certified applications over at the Department of Labor, under NAFTA TAA, it is now 111,000 people in this country that have been certified to receive that assistance, taxpayer subsidy dollars, because they have lost their jobs due to NAFTA. This says nothing about what is happening inside Mexico and I could talk about that for an hour and I will not.

Ms. ROS-LEHTINEN. Why don't we go through those really quickly, Marcy, if you could.

Ms. KAPTUR. All right.

Ms. ROS-LEHTINEN. The rest of the charts.

Ms. KAPTUR. If we could put up the chart next of Mexico. The one that is on the ground. Yes.

This gives you a feel for, in some ways, like our own trade deficit, if you look what happened in Mexico, there is a debt crisis every

5 or 6 years. And you see where NAFTA is signed there. There were trade surpluses that preceded NAFTA's signing. Once it was signed, the trade deficits have gotten deeper every year—$15.4 billion, $16.2 billion with Mexico.

And, Tim, if you could put up the other graphic of Canada, you will note also that our trade deficit with Canada has doubled. The Canadian situation is a little bit different than the Mexican situation. But you can see, if you look at the trade surplus that existed with Mexico, $1.7 billion in the blue arrow, that is now translated last year into a $16-billion deficit with our country and with Canada we have doubled in terms of the deficit situation. So we are talking about real lost jobs in this country and then there are internals going on in both Mexico and Canada that are not written about very much but which are very, very important.

The automotive sector is absolutely the most significant one in terms of U.S.-Mexico trade. And I guess about $15 billion of that trade deficit relates to automotive. It is interesting how the Administration—and more than one Administration, by the way, has done this—they always talk about exports. Exports, exports, exports. Well, in the checkbook there is also the debit side of the ledger, not just the asset side.

And if you look at pre-NAFTA, the trade represented by the arrows there, both in cars and trucks, you will see that we did have a deficit with Mexico at that point. But in automobiles, it has now doubled. And in trucks, it has gotten eight times worse. Eight times worse. So our theory that, no, this was not the development of a consumer market in Mexico, this is the development of an export platform through which goods are outsourced from this country into Mexico as well as other countries. And then you turn back into this country. The Mexican people have not been able to improve their standard of living with the peso devaluation and all the rest and so what you have is a very serious trade imbalance that hurts millions of people across the continent, including well over probably three-quarters of a million directly in our own Nation.

I will submit the majority of testimony——

Ms. ROS-LEHTINEN. We will be glad to submit that in the record.

Ms. KAPTUR [continuing]. for the record, Madam Chair, and one recommendation I would make is that the Committee seriously look at our NAFTA Accountability Act. It is a very measured way of forcing a report card on NAFTA's various provisions so we can look at the information objectively, repair it where it is not working, and not permit expansion until we fix what is wrong with this agreement.

[The prepared statement of Ms. Kaptur appears in the appendix.]

Ms. ROS-LEHTINEN. Thank you so much, Congresswoman. Thank you to the panelists as well.

I will begin, first, with Mr. Manzullo, who will be followed by Mr. Hilliard.

Mr. MANZULLO. Thank you very much. I just have three short comments. Then, unfortunately, I have to go back to my office for another meeting.

I think when you look at NAFTA in terms of simplification, I always call this a good 10–4. Products that were manufactured have been manufactured in the United States. They were sent to Mexico and paid, on the average, a 10-percent tariff. Products manufactured in Mexico are sent to the United States and paid, on the average, a 4-percent tariff. And the big 10–4 is that under NAFTA, they would be reduced to zero. That really is the basis of NAFTA. It is a reduction of the tariff rates between the countries to zero. Before NAFTA, Mexico had a tariff rate of 2½ times that of the United States. That is really what NAFTA is about. It is reducing those tariff rates.

The second thing is, what NAFTA did—and Ambassador Shapiro pointed it out very succinctly—back in 1982, when Mexico had a crisis, they lost six-tenths of 1 percent of their GDP and yet they threw up their import barriers and U.S. exports to Mexico fell by 35 percent. Then in 1983, the Mexican GDP had another hit of 4.2 percent decrease. And, again, the Mexican Government threw up their shields and American exports reduced by 25 percent. And then in 1995, the biggest crisis of all when Mexican GDP fell by 7 percent because of the NAFTA agreement, U.S. exports to Mexico fell by only 13 percent. So I think, if you look at in terms of the general philosophy of NAFTA and the purpose for which it was intended, it is good. It is making sense because, with the latest problem in Mexico, if we did not have NAFTA, they would have cut off the borders and we would have had a lot of American products that would have not have been able to go to Mexico.

I guess we could talk about trade deficits all we want but we have to ask the question, would the trade deficit have been any greater without NAFTA. We do not know these things and all I can do is I can take a look at manufacturing sector by manufacturing sector. I represent a congressional district that has over 1500 manufacturing facilities. We export everything. We have the No. 1 dairy in the county in the State of Illinois, the fastener capital of the world, things that lock, snap, hinges, bolts and things. Those things get shipped to Mexico that are used for assembling Mexican automobile plants and then they come back to the United States, what we call imports here. So it is a huge picture.

But here we are in the United States. We are talking about NAFTA as causing the loss of all these jobs and when I talk to the employers, they cannot find workers. Unemployment is at 4, 4½ percent. If we have lost 800,000 workers, where are these workers going to come from? Manufacturers are desperately trying to find people to carry on these jobs. So I just want to make a comment that, from a practical aspect and looking very simply at NAFTA, this appears to be working.

And, Marcy, I appreciate what you are showing here. But those cars, before NAFTA, we only sent about 2900 cars. Then after 1993, we are sending 46,000. And, sure, they are sending a lot more back to us but one thing this could never take into consideration is how those fasteners and bolts and hinges and screws and pins and all these little things that are manufactured by big and small manufacturers all find their way south of the border and suddenly they come back up to us and, for some reason, after NAFTA, we are at some of the lowest unemployment in history. So to say that American jobs have been lost on NAFTA—sure, some have lost but I think, on the whole, we have done OK.

Ms. KAPTUR. Mr. Manzullo, how would you respond to the 111,000 Americans that have now applied for TAA and received it? They should take their medicine and swallow it?

Mr. MANZULLO. Well, it is not so much due to what has happened in Mexico, Marcy. I have an article here, for example, that was in the Washington Times. It is a little bit dated but it talks about some of the people that applied to TAA. Some figures show it at 19,000. Some show it at 51,000. But I think you have to take a look at the net loss and then ask yourself would these jobs have been lost whether or not NAFTA went into effect anyway. I mean, we simply have to ask that question. I do not think they would be because the purpose of NAFTA was to reduce barriers to make it cheaper for American goods to be sold to Mexico. And, as Mr. Shapiro stated, that is exactly what is happening.

Ms. KAPTUR. Well, I think, with all due respect to the gentleman, I think you hit the nail on the head when you said the fasteners are sent to Mexico. They are put in vehicles that are sent back to the United States and they are u-turn goods there, not the development of a true consumer market in Mexico. I think you hit the nail on the head.

Mr. MANZULLO. Thank you.

Ms. ROS-LEHTINEN. Thank you.

Ms. KAPTUR. You hit the fastener on the head.

Ms. ROS-LEHTINEN. Mr. Manzullo and Congressman Kaptur, in the interest of time, because in the third panel we have two folks who need to make their flight, I am going to try my best to adhere to the 5-minute rule.

Mr. Hilliard.

Mr. HILLIARD. Thank you very much, Madam Chairman. I want to direct a question to Ambassador Shapiro.

I notice on page three of this statement you said that NAFTA has played a vital role in helping trade expansion strengthen the U.S. economy. I also heard during your testimony—and correct me if I am wrong—that you attribute our good economy and our low unemployment rate to NAFTA when you were talking about the statement that Mr. Bonior made. And with our trade deficit being what it is with Mexico and with the theory that economists have that for every billion dollars in trade deficit, so many jobs are lost to our economy, I would just like to know how you reconcile your testimony and your statement with that well-known economic theory.

Mr. SHAPIRO. Mr. Hilliard, essentially along the lines of to what Congressman Manzullo was referring. We have a very strong economy right now, particularly in some of the industrial States.

Mr. HILLIARD. Because of NAFTA?

Mr. SHAPIRO. No, no. Because of a lot of things that we are doing right in our economy. NAFTA is only——

Mr. HILLIARD. You think that NAFTA is one of them?

Mr. SHAPIRO. NAFTA is a positive. I would not say it is a huge positive. I would say it is a positive. It is part of our overall trade strategy.

I would say, basically, in response to Ms. Kaptur's point, we will confess—we count exports and imports differently because you can count exports and you know when you export something how many jobs it creates. With imports—and my testimony goes through this—some imports go into domestic production. Some imports come in in short supply situations. Some imports complement production. There are all kinds of reasons why not every import can be equated with a job loss.

But the other thing I wanted to say about the trade deficit—and I know we all think about trade deficits—you look at Japan, you look at a country where you have chronic trade deficits, and I think, over the years, you can say you have a market access problem. If your trade deficit changes sharply, as this one did in 1 year, I think you have to look for a different explanation and the explanation in this case was, the Mexican economy went into a recession three times deeper than the last one we had. A very deep recession. Their currency collapsed and that changed the trade balance. I would much prefer to have our economy and a trade deficit with Mexico than their recession. And so there are a lot of things that go into this.

But one point I just wanted to make, with the Chair's indulgence—because some of these numbers can be interesting——

Ms. ROS-LEHTINEN. Indulge you until the red light comes on.

Mr. SHAPIRO. Thank you, Madam Chair.

We heard a lot from NAFTA opponents about how investment was going to go into Mexico to drain investment from the United States. So I think this number is relevant. The total foreign investment in Mexico in 1995 was $7 billion. $2.1 billion of foreign investment from the United States into Mexico. In contrast, our country had $60 billion of foreign investment here and our total investment, three-quarters of which was business, was $1.1 trillion.

Now, I think that illustrates some of the problems that the opponents' numbers have here. We turn out to be a generator of investment in the United States and a magnet for other people's investment. There is no investment flight to Mexico and so I use that as just one example of the fact that some of these numbers need to be looked at quite closely on both sides.

Ms. ROS-LEHTINEN. Thank you so much.

Mr. Brady.

Mr. BRADY. Thank you, Madam Chairwoman.

I agree. The numbers are a little confusing. I know that last year, 1996, our exports grew some 23 percent. Mexico's imports grew less than that, about 18 percent. I guess it depends upon the timeframe and the descriptions that they are using to crunch the numbers to make their story.

But today, earlier, we heard assertions that poverty in Mexico and low wages along the border, environmental issues, all have occurred and, in part, occurred because of NAFTA. But as a delegate from Texas where we have been dealing with environmental issues for decades and decades, low wages, non-existent wages, where we have dealt with immigration and poverty in Mexico, we see NAFTA as the potential to increase those wages to try to build an economy in Mexico to help to shape the environment along the border, all of which, without the dollars that drive them, we are, just like in inner cities, going to have trouble handling it.

So I would ask the Ambassador, do you believe that NAFTA is the cause of poverty in Mexico—low wages, environmental problems along the border States?

Mr. SHAPIRO. Obviously, I do not. I think there are some serious conditions in Mexico that will take years to overcome. I think NAFTA can contribute positively to that. The Mexican Government has started to contribute positively, too. I think we had a setback. Both NAFTA countries certainly had a setback from the peso crisis, although the recovery has been good in the last year. But I think that this is a longer-term process. I would say on the environmental side, we all know that the conditions at the border are not acceptable in any way.

But if you look at some of the infrastructure projects that we have only begun to fund through the NAD Bank and through the border commission that we set up, you will find wastewater treatment projects on a scale that we have never had before. The San Diego facility—and I talk about it in my statement—will, we believe, for the first time in 50 years, provide a permanent solution to the sewage problem in Tijuana. We all know that these environmental problems were years in the making and it is going to take some time to improve the situation. We also know that even in our own country it takes time to deal with some difficult environmental problems—cleaning rivers, dealing with toxic wastes.

The question really remains whether there is any evidence that we or the Mexicans would be any way better off without NAFTA and without some of the cooperative efforts that we have put in place. I have detailed them in the statement. I cannot go through them all. But I think all of us—and I know the opponents of NAFTA feel the same way—you have to ask yourself whether the situation would be somehow better without the framework of cooperation and the framework of expanded trade that we have put in place so far.

Mr. BRADY. Thank you, sir.

Thank you, Madam Chairwoman.

Ms. ROS-LEHTINEN. Thank you so much. And thanks to Mr. Clement who has been so patiently awaiting. Thank you, Bob.

Mr. CLEMENT. Thank you, Madam Chairman.

And, Ambassador Shapiro, it is a pleasure to have you here, and Ms. Vargo and Congresswoman Marcy Kaptur. And I might say for her, she truly represents her people at home. It is a pleasure to serve with you, Marcy.

Ms. KAPTUR. Thank you.

Mr. CLEMENT. This question is to the Ambassador and Ms. Vargo, but please feel free to comment, Congresswoman, and please keep your remarks brief, if you could, because I have three questions.

My first question. There are a number of companies, including my home State of Tennessee, who have become frustrated with the high occurrence of cargo theft and truck hijacking while operating in Mexico. Is the Administration currently working with Mexican officials to protect these drivers and cargo?

Mr. SHAPIRO. Congressman, I can say that we are working on this problem. But I would like to give you a fuller answer from the Department of Transportation, who has been doing more of this.

Mr. CLEMENT. Is that the same answer for you, Ms. Vargo?

Ms. VARGO. Yes.

Mr. CLEMENT. OK.

My second question. Public Citizens Global Trade Watch reports that more than 600,000 Americans have lost their jobs due to NAFTA. Are these figures correct? If so, what more can we do to stem this job loss and protect and to create new jobs for Americans?

Mr. SHAPIRO. I think the 600,000 figure is completely fallacious. I would guess it is based simply on multiplying the trade deficit by a certain number of jobs in a way that I do not think is representative of anything. I know some of the opponents of NAFTA have used 100,000 because those are the number of workers that have been identified for trade adjustment assistance. Even those, I would note, and any number of thousands is of concern, but even those, I would note, refers to all people who are affected by the trade and not necessarily by NAFTA. I am told that only 5,000 of those have come forward for the training that results. But certainly the 600,000 number has no basis.

Ms. Vargo.

Ms. VARGO. I would like to just add one thing to that because so much of the concern about NAFTA seems to be reflected in the trade balance and I think it is important to point out that at any given time, the biggest determinant of a trade balance, more than anything, is going to be the relative economic growth rate for the two countries. When your economy is growing, you are going to have a demand for imports and you are going to pull them in. If you are growing faster than your trading partner, you are likely to develop a situation where temporarily you will run a deficit. When the deficits are chronic, when they seem structural, you get concerned. But that is not the case that we have with Mexico right now, given the depth of the recession that they have.

The easiest way to point out this disconnect between a trade balance and a job impact is just to look at the last year. Mexico made an incredible swing in its trade balance, Madam Chairman, on the order of $20, $30 billion. And yet they suffered over 1.6 million unemployed in that recession.

By contrast, you are correct, our trade deficit did increase with Mexico and with Canada. Yet Canada has an unemployment rate of 10 percent. We have one of our lowest unemployment rates in, what, almost a decade? We have created roughly 9 million new jobs since NAFTA went into place. So it is important that we not fixate on the deficit.

Mr. CLEMENT. Thank you.

Ms. ROS-LEHTINEN. OK.

Ms. KAPTUR. Madam Chair, might I respond to that?

Mr. CLEMENT. All right.

Ms. KAPTUR. Does the gentleman have an additional question?

Mr. CLEMENT. Yes, I have one more question. Let me ask the one more question and then you can respond to both.

Fourteen months ago, the Administration delayed implementation of NAFTA provisions that would allow Mexican motor carriers to operate anywhere in California, in New Mexico, Arizona and Texas. It is my understanding that the safety and security concerns that led to this decision have not been resolved and remain just as serious. Is the Administration considering removing current restrictions?

Mr. SHAPIRO. I think, Mr. Clement, there were strong feelings on both sides of the issue when we made the decision in December, 1995. And over the course of the 14 months, the Department of Transportation and Customs working with the affected States, we believe, have made substantial progress in improving our enforcement efforts along the border and improving the safety regimes of all our NAFTA partners. We will not open the border until we are satisfied on the question of safety and we have made no decision at this time. But we do recognize the need to resolve the issue and we are hopeful and hope that we can do it in a way that does not in any way threaten the safety or security of anyone.

I want to, if I could, submit for the record, Madam Chairman, a description of everything that has happened in the last 14 months.

Ms. ROS-LEHTINEN. We will be glad to enter it.

Mr. SHAPIRO. And supplement the record in that way.

Ms. VARGO. I think you covered the main points.

Ms. KAPTUR. I just wanted to place on the record, if I might, Congressman Clement, listening to the Ambassador—one of the troubling aspects of NAFTA for me as a citizen of this country and a Member of Congress is the short shrift that is given by this Administration to those in our country who, in fact, have lost their jobs and, Mr. Ambassador, lost them to outsourcing to Mexico. Whether you are talking about Thompson Electronics in Indiana, tomato growers in Florida, Delphia workers in Warren, Ohio, the Administration has to stop the denial.

We have thousands, tens of thousands, of people in this country that have lost their jobs. Now, big people admit mistakes and if we are going to get this to work right, you cannot not recognize the people in this country that have been harmed, with all due respect. And I think that NAFTA is such a major blueprint, it could not have been done perfectly at first. But to be insensitive to the people of this country that are hurting—and, by the way, you mentioned not taking advantage of training. I should give you some of the letters I have received from around the country of the kind of training that is being offered. If the Department of Congress cannot be more sensitive to our own citizenry, how can we hope to be sensitive to the people of Mexico that are being hurt by this agreement?

I think, on the job front, the evidence is very clear. On the trucking issue, let me just say—and I am sure others have stated this for the record—that we only actually check one of every hundred trucks coming over those borders and one of the provisions in our NAFTA Accountability Act has to do with the trucking provisions. We are very concerned about inspection, particularly in view of the drug trade and some of it flies over, it does not get trucked over, as you know; but also the certification of drivers, the drug testing for those drivers and the types of safety equipment that are going to be necessary to drive on our roads. I am very worried about what the Administration is going to do in this area, if anything, and so I am glad the Congressman asked the question.

Ms. ROS-LEHTINEN. Thank you so much.

And for the last Member to ask questions of this panel, thank you so much, Mr. Sherman, from California.

Mr. SHERMAN. First, I want to compliment you not only on your presentation but on really cool charts and particularly illustrative, the chart that talked about our trade deficit worldwide because during the 1980's, the foreign policy establishment told us that our trade deficit was mostly our fault because we were running a large U.S. budget deficit that led to the import of capital, higher U.S. dollars, you know the routine. Well, we have cut the Federal deficit and we have enlarged the trade deficit simultaneously. And so I am waiting for the foreign policy establishment to tell us, once again, with a different reason, why the trade deficit has nothing to do with our trading partners or trading relationship.

I want to focus my questions on Chapter 11 of NAFTA and address them to the Ambassador and put forth the following scenario. Under NAFTA, if a country expropriates foreign investments, it is actionable. The company that lost the investment is entitled to be compensated and it is even detailed as to what currency and with interest and all that.

So if, for some reason, in a particular country there was an expropriation, that country should compensate the party that lost property. But if they failed to do so, would one of the other signatories to NAFTA have any liability at all?

Mr. SHAPIRO. Why don't you answer?

Ms. VARGO. OK.

Mr. SHAPIRO. I always turn to the person who knows the answer.

Ms. VARGO. Now, the way that provision works is the investor has to have a dispute with the government, such as over an expropriation, and actually that provision was written in order to make the Mexican Government subject to binding arbitration. The way the Mexican law works, a foreign investor cannot ask their home government for help in any case that takes the Government of Mexico to the Mexican courts. So we said, "Fine. We would rather U.S. investors in Mexico have the option to use binding arbitration than to go to Mexican court anyway." And if Mexico were to fail to honor such an award, it would be a violation of the NAFTA. I think, at that point, the U.S. Government would step in. Up until then, it is a private matter between the investor and the Mexican Government.

We have not yet had that situation. But should it arise, the U.S. Government would be able to take the Mexican Government to dispute settlement for failure to honor the obligations of the agreement, which could allow us to put pressure on the Government of Mexico (including the withdrawal of trade benefit to provide compensation).

Mr. SHERMAN. The people from my district are not looking for an opportunity to provide compensation.

Ms. VARGO. Short answer—we are not going to be responsible to pay a company if they do not get financial compensation from the Mexican Government.

Mr. SHERMAN. So we have your personal assurance, you are absolutely certain——

Ms. VARGO. Yes.

Mr. SHERMAN. The U.S. Government will not be liable for a single dollar of property expropriated in Mexico under NAFTA.

Ms. VARGO. It is not part of the agreement, no.

Mr. SHERMAN. A related question goes back to the issues of truck safety that Bob brought up and that is, I represent a border State. I am particularly concerned that trucks that are too large and too old, driven by drivers that have no particularly effective regulation, are going to be causing automobile accidents. And there is no effective way to make sure that there is proper insurance. Now, monetary compensation does not really compensate for a tragedy like that. But is there any provision in NAFTA that would have the U.S. Government step in and pay someone who was terribly mangled by a poorly trained and poorly licensed driver from Mexico on our streets driving there pursuant to NAFTA?

Mr. SHAPIRO. Well, Congressman, let me say, first of all, that in the detailed material that I would like to submit to the Committee, much of what the Department of Transportation has been working on in the last 14 months is an effort to ensure that no Mexican driver who ever drives in the border States, if the border is open, no Mexican driver would be any less qualified in every respect than his U.S. counterpart. Similarly, that the vehicles would be held to the same standard. And this has been work that has been going on for, as I say, more than a year in very detailed ways to assure that this comes about.

Now, with respect to the exact question you have asked in terms of liability, I do not think so. But I would have to check.

Mr. SHERMAN. If the Chairwoman would indulge me—it would have an awful lot more credibility if the Administration would put the U.S. Government's money where its mouth is and say that anyone who suffers damage as a result of one of these NAFTA truck cargos, who is able to establish that either the driver did not meet U.S. standards or the truck did not meet U.S. standards, would, if they could not recover from the trucking company, be able to recover from the Federal Government. To expose the people of my State to risks, it at least ought to call for compensation. And if you are correct and there is not a single Mexican driver or a single Mexican truck on the roads of California that fails to meet our standards, of course such a provision would cost you nothing.

Mr. SHAPIRO. I appreciate the thought and I will discuss it with others. I am correct in saying that that is the goal for which the DOT has been working for 14 months so that if we reach the point where we have concluded that the border can be opened, that safety levels of both vehicles and drivers would be at that level, that, of course, requires much different kinds of inspection facilities and intensified inspection recordkeeping and any number of other things that are detailed in here.

Ms. KAPTUR. Congressman Sherman, a 15-second comment, if I might. It was interesting that during the peso bail-out negotiations that the taxpayers of the United States became the insurance company for Mexico and there was a guarantee given then, unprecedented, no vote of Congress. Maybe they could do the same in the area of trucking to assure that the drivers in your State are also insured by the Treasury of the United States.

Ms. ROS-LEHTINEN. Thank you, Marcy, Regina and Ira. Thank you for excellent testimony. We really appreciate your patience and thank you so much for enlightening us on your views. We look forward to having you back when we do our followup hearing in July.

Our third panel is headed by Ron Carey, general president of the International Brotherhood of Teamsters. Fresh out of the Marines in 1956, Mr. Carey went on to work as a UPS driver and 2 years later was elected shop steward. This began a long career working for labor rights, which included serving as the president of one of the largest UPS locals in the country and the negotiations for the first 25-year and pension at UPS for its members. We appreciate Mr. Carey being here with us and we know that a number of our panelists have planes to catch and we will try to adhere to the 5-minute rule.

Following Mr. Carey is Mr. Willard Workman, vice-president for the International Policy of the U.S. Chamber of Commerce. Mr. Workman is responsible for the formulation and the implementation of the Chamber's policy positions on international economic and trade issues. He also serves as vice-president for the Center of International Private Enterprise, a Chamber-affiliated group dedicated to assisting emerging private sector and market-oriented groups in the developing world. Previously, he served as special negotiator for the International Trade Controls at the U.S. Department of State and also as director for strategic planning and policy in the Bureau of Export Administration.

Our final witness today is Mr. Paul DiMare, who owns and operates DiMare's Company operations. His companies operate in my congressional district of Homestead, Florida, as well as two other Florida cities, Ruskin and Tampa, as well as St. John Island in South Carolina and Boston and in Indio, California. Mr. DiMare has been an industry activist since his early days in our State of Florida. He is past president of the Florida Tomato Exchange and the Florida Tomato Committee. He is currently chairman of the Florida Farmers and Suppliers Coalition.

We welcome all three of you gentlemen for being here today.

Mr. Carey.

STATEMENT OF RON CAREY, GENERAL PRESIDENT, INTERNATIONAL BROTHERHOOD OF TEAMSTERS

Mr. CAREY. Thank you.

On behalf of the 1.4 million members of the Teamster Union, I want to thank you for the opportunity for my testimony today.

The NAFTA trade deal, and I use the term "deal," has left a clear trail of winners and losers. Multinational corporations have won big by exploiting Mexican workers and destroying good jobs in the United States. The result—working families have been the losers. Now the Administration is preparing to implement the trucking part of NAFTA. If that happens, even more workers will become victims of this trade deal as jobs are eliminated and real wages are eroded.

As you know, in December 1995, the Clinton Administration delayed the trucking part of NAFTA because of concerns over highway safety, the environment, and American jobs. Fourteen months later, those problems still exist. Currently, trucks from Mexico are confined to a 20- or 30-mile strip along the border where freight is picked up by American drivers for delivery in the United States. The trucking part of NAFTA would give unsafe trucks from Mexico immediate access to the four border States and to all of the United States in the year 2000.

Before I continue on with my very brief testimony, I have asked Bob Nicklas, a member of my staff, to give you a brief review or view of his visit in February to the border crossing at Laredo, Texas. This area is one of the busiest entry points for Mexican trucks into the United States.

Bob.

STATEMENT OF BOB NICKLAS, LEGISLATIVE DEPARTMENT, INTERNATIONAL BROTHERHOOD OF TEAMSTERS

Mr. NICKLAS. The photos you are about to see were taken on February 12, 1997.

Ms. ROS-LEHTINEN. Sir, if it would be possible, just to use—right. Because the transcriber needs to have it go through her earpiece.

Mr. NICKLAS. The photos you are about to see were taken on February 12 and February 13 of this year.

Can everybody on the panel see?

This is a picture of the four custom inspection booths at Laredo's downtown Lincoln Bridge. About 4500 trucks a day cross into the United States at Laredo and these four booths right here handle almost all of the traffic. The average inspection time is 3 to 4 minutes. In that amount of time, Customs must enforce 600 regulations for 60 different agencies. That includes whether the driver has a legitimate border crossing card, whether or not they have adequate insurance, how long they have been driving, and, of course, what is inside the truck, including drugs.

This is a more panoramic view of that same inspection area. These are the Custom booths back here. This is the truck inspection area in the front photo. You will notice a couple of different things. There is only one scale for weighing 4500 trucks a day. You will notice another thing, which is that no truck is being inspected. This is the area where the cars are parked that would prevent any truck from actually going through the inspection area. You will also notice that the inspection area is totally removed from the flow of traffic and that the consequence of the first three things is that the trucks are totally bypassing the inspection area.

This is a photo of the lower level of the same Customs compound and what I would like you to focus on is this center area where right now you see no activity. While we were standing taking photos, several Department of Public Service personnel noticed that I was taking photos and that I was standing with a former Customs inspector. Within minutes, this lone officer right here took these highway cones and set up a very impromptu inspection area for our benefit. About 10 minutes later, the lone officer was gone and the traffic continued to flow through the border uninspected.

We went back to Laredo to the same spot the next morning, just to make sure that we could believe what we saw. And, as this photo shows again, no trucks are being inspected. There are vehicles parked in the inspection area and the trucks are going right around them.

44-878 98 - 2

The short moral to the story is that standards mean nothing and the inspection of trucks means nothing, in terms of what is inside them, unless we have strong enforcement, and we do not.

Mr. CAREY. Thank you, Bob.

Ms. ROS-LEHTINEN. Mr. Carey.

Mr. CAREY. What you saw in these photos sums up what I consider the phony promises about NAFTA and these promises are being made to working families all over this country. We were promised that NAFTA would create employment. But more than 420,000 jobs, American jobs, have been lost since it took effect in 1994. We were promised greater prosperity, but our trade surplus with Mexico has turned into the largest trade deficit with that country in our history. And isn't it ironic that I heard testimony where every time you mention trade deficit, there is hedging, "Do not talk about that, that is not really the issue here." But the trade deficit does have a meaningful impact in terms of jobs, in terms of this economy.

We were told that NAFTA would improve wages. But big corporations have used it to drag down the standards of living for many working families. We were told NAFTA would help workers, but the wages have gone down since NAFTA was passed. Now we are being told that under the trucking part of NAFTA, our roads will be safe, drugs will be stopped at the border and working people will benefit. It was a lie when NAFTA was passed and it is a lie now. There is no enforcement at the border. These trucks are a ticking time bomb on our highways. They are a ready-made pipeline to bring more drugs into our schools and into our neighborhoods. The NAFTA trucking provisions serve no purpose except to let American trucking companies replace hard-working middle class workers with low-wage exploited Mexican workers.

This government is supposed to represent American workers. If that holds true, then the NAFTA trucking delay should be made permanent and trucking provisions should be renegotiated to protect working families on both sides of the border.

Thank you very much.

[The prepared statement of Mr. Carey appears in the appendix.]

Ms. ROS-LEHTINEN. Thank you so much, Mr. Carey. We appreciate it.

Mr. Workman.

STATEMENT OF WILLARD A. WORKMAN, VICE-PRESIDENT, INTERNATIONAL DIVISION, U.S. CHAMBER OF COMMERCE

Mr. WORKMAN. Thank you, Madam Chair. You have my statement. I would like to submit it for the record.

Ms. ROS-LEHTINEN. Yes. We will submit all of the statements.

Mr. WORKMAN. Then I will briefly summarize my comments.

First, I would like, for the Subcommittee's benefit, to put NAFTA in context. Not many people in this country realize it, but trade over the past 25 years has become increasingly important to our economy. In 1970, trade—that is not only exports but also imports—believe it or not, some people in the import markets also have jobs—imports do, in certain instances, create jobs—but, at any rate, in 1970 trade accounted for 13 percent of the U.S. Gross Domestic Product. In 1995, it accounted for 30 percent. By the year

2010, it will probably be on the order of at least 40 to 45 percent. So we are looking at something that, like it or not, we are in the global economy and it is going to have an impact on us in a lot of ways—some of which we may be able to foresee, some of which we may not.

In my membership—and I come from an outfit that represents an underlying membership of about three million companies, 96 percent of them are companies that employ less than 100 workers, 71 percent of them are companies that employ less than ten workers, only 4 percent of them are what would be classified by some as big business and, the way we counted it at the Chamber, big business is someone that employs more than 100 workers. So whether that meets the definition of a multinational, I am not sure.

But, in any event, in our membership things that we have seen since NAFTA went into place, since the Uruguay Round Agreement was adopted, there has been a remarkable shift in the way the small- and medium-sized companies in our membership look at trade and how trade can affect them, either positively or negatively. They have looked at some studies, and I will be glad to provide the copies of the studies for you, but, to summarize them—companies that are engaged in trade, principally those that export, their workers' productivity is, on average, 20 percent higher than those who do not work in trade or do not engage in trade. The wages are 15 percent higher in exporting companies than in non-exporting companies. A company that engages in trade, particularly a small- or medium-sized company, is 9 percent less likely to go bankrupt in a given year. Their employment rate, among exporting companies, is 20 percent faster than among non-exporting companies.

That being said, and the thing that is really interesting to me, looking at some of our small companies in the membership, in 1987, only about one in ten manufacturers with fewer than 100 workers exported at all. In 1992, one in five did.

Another interesting point to make, and I think this has some significant implications because we have had some so-called protectionist companies in our membership and the attitude is changing significantly—between 1994 and 1996, the share of small- and medium-sized companies that got 10 percent or more of their sales from exports doubled from 27 percent to 51 percent. That is a remarkable shift. In talking to these people on an individual basis, they point almost without exception to one thing about why did they even get involved in international trade and they say NAFTA. A lot of them had, in the first year of NAFTA, incredible positive experiences. In the second year of NAFTA, during the peso crisis, they were sobered, to say the least. By the third year of NAFTA, eight out of ten of them are back in Mexico, in Canada, and, interestingly enough, are looking forward to the rest of the hemisphere. So I thought I would bring that to the Committee's attention.

Again, you have my testimony and I would close just by making one point. I think it was Congresswoman Kaptur who earlier said that NAFTA is the blueprint for the hemisphere. I have been to the Mercusur countries as recently as last November and I can assure you that NAFTA is not the blueprint for what is going to happen in this hemisphere. We missed that opportunity. When the Clinton

Administration refused to take the fast track trade negotiating authority that a Democratic Congress had given to Ronald Reagan and to George Bush and we sat on our hands for the past 2 years, the rest of the hemisphere has moved on. The Mercusur countries—Paraguay, Uruguay, Brazil and Argentina—constitute 60 percent of the GDP of South America. Chile is already an associate member. Bolivia is already an associate member. So we are not going to have NAFTA, as much as we in American business would like to have seen NAFTA as the blueprint. This clearly is going to be the situation in the future, if we get the negotiating authority, where it is going to be a negotiation between trading blocks. So it is not going to be NAFTA as the hub and Chile and Argentina and Brazil are spokes added to that hub. That is not the way it is going to work.

So, in our view, we have already had a missed opportunity. We think that NAFTA works. As I said in my testimony, we would give the agreement an "A." We would give the governments—not only the U.S. Government but the Mexican Government and the Canadian Government—a "B" in terms of implementation.

There is an issue with trucking. We know there is an issue with trucking. I find it interesting that the State governments that are responsible for highway safety, the Governors of Arizona, New Mexico, Texas and California last December wrote to the President saying that they were comfortable with the procedures that had been put in place and to lift the 20-mile ban.

Finally, I would bring to your attention another item and then I will leave my summary. NAFTA provides for tariff reduction. In certain areas, we have seen a tremendous boom on all sides of the board—Canadian, U.S. and Mexican—in the initial early harvest, if you will, in certain sectors. We used the tariff acceleration provisions in the old U.S.-Canada Free Trade Agreement to both countries' benefit. They have never been exercised to our Members' satisfaction in NAFTA. We would like to see all governments go back, look at that and, rather than having to wait until the year 2010 for full tariff reduction or lowering, let's see if we cannot speed it up.

Thank you, Madam.

[The prepared statement of Mr. Workman appears in the appendix.]

Ms. ROS-LEHTINEN. Thank you so much, Mr. Workman, for your testimony.

I am honored to have Mr. DiMare here with us, a constituent from my congressional district who has been very active in the agricultural sector of our State and of our Nation and also in the audience is Mr. James Humble, who has represented many property owners, especially in the South 80 area, and we welcome both of you. And, Mr. DiMare, we look forward to your testimony.

STATEMENT OF PAUL J. DIMARE, FARMER AND OWNER, DIMARE HOMESTEAD, INC., (ALSO REPRESENTING THE FLORIDA TOMATO EXCHANGE)

Mr. DIMARE. Thank you, Madam Chairperson. I feel privileged that you have asked me here today.

I sat in my chair and listened to a lot of the statements by mostly government people, people working for associations that do not represent American people, the American worker. I am a small businessperson. My family is the fourth generation of farming in the United States. Came from Italy. I have seen something happen to this country that I do not believe people realize. American jobs are disappearing. Good-paying jobs.

I have listened to all the statistics and they are the most phony statistics I have ever heard. When they sold NAFTA they said, "We are going to create jobs." It was a win-win. Win for Mexico, win for the United States. They never sold it on the basis that we were going to have a deficit with Mexico. You could not sell that to the American Congress. How could you tell them that we were going to have a deficit and that we were going to have a trade agreement with a country that is a Third World country? Impossible. So you sold it on the basis that we were going to have a win-win.

We had a positive trading balance with Mexico previous to NAFTA. Always had a trading surplus. We turned the first year to a $16-billion trade deficit. Using the President's numbers, that is a loss of 300,000 jobs. Those are the numbers he sold to you people. I listened to Carla Hills at every hearing that was on C–SPAN. Those are the numbers that they used. "We are going to create 20,000 jobs for every single billion dollars in trade." Well, you lose them the same way as you gain them when you have a deficit and people forgot about deficits in this country. We have $180-billion trade deficit this year. We are now $1.9 trillion in trade deficits since 1973.

General Motors is now the largest single employer in Mexico with 26 plants. Eighty-six thousand people they employ. Our great General Motors. This has been an escape. Every trade agreement this country has made has been an escape for the multinationals to move out of this country and set up deals in foreign countries with slave wages and no regulations and human rights violations and child labor. What kind of a country are we that we want to be an affluent society and earn good wages but we want to buy products from people that are paying their people nothing? Is that what people want?

I want to make $40 an hour, or $47.50 is what General Motors' wage base is with their benefits and thank God it is, but we want to buy shirts from people that make 20 cents an hour? You cannot live in that kind of society. Eventually, you will not have a job and that is exactly what is happening to this country. We are losing our manufacturing base.

I told somebody if they shut down the whole agricultural deal in Florida, Florida will be hurt. I will find something else to do as a person because that is the way I was brought up. But I want to tell you something. As an American citizen, if you congressional people do not do something about trade in this country—and NAFTA is only one of the problems that we have—if you do not sit there and honestly look at it with a true picture instead of listening to these politicians that are coming here from NAFTA and the State Department, I do not know who they represent. But they do not represent these American people that I come from.

And when Senator Dole went and ran in New Hampshire and all of a sudden he came up and said, "Geez, I did not know American jobs and the economy was a problem," he found out it was a problem. If you are sitting there and lost that job that Congresswoman Kaptur talked about—whether it was 100,000, 10,000 or two million—which there are probably about three million jobs right now because if you multiply the $180-billion trade deficit we had this year it is over three million jobs lost—that is after you take out the ones gained for imports—this is the net. I created so many from exports and we forget about imports. This is the net number. You have lost over three million jobs this year in this country that are high-paying jobs. How are you going to replace them? Service jobs? Sorry.

Service jobs pay one third of manufacturing jobs. We have gone, since 1973, 31 percent of our total labor force in manufacturing to 15 percent. That is a total disgrace. You cannot run a country on service jobs.

The Labor Department has just announced the next largest growth job in the United States for the next 10 years. Do you know what it is? Cashiers. Oh, that is a big-paying job. I am going to be a cashier. Isn't that a wonderful minimum-wage job? Where is our base of manufacturing? You cannot run a country—God forbid we would have to go to war again. Where are we going to make all these products?

We have turned over the tail sections and the landing sections of our 737's and 747's to China to make for Boeing. Isn't this dangerous? Isn't this a national disgrace that a country that will probably be our next adversary in a war, China, is going to make planes for Boeing? And we have turned over the technological knowledge in the tool and die industry to these people. You people are not scared of that? Are you naive to think that the Americans are always going to survive? There has been no country in the world that has ever been No. 1 that you could knock down to two or three and never come back again. Remember that. There have been some tremendous countries. We are a very young country. Do not ever let this country go. And, believe me, every country is biting at our tail to put us down.

Mexico, of all countries, that is the worst bunch of bandits that I have ever dealt with. Not the Mexican people, the Mexican politicians. They are crooks through and through. They are involved so deep into dope and corruption. We did something for who, the Mexican people? If you wanted to do something for Mexico, why didn't you put a minimum wage in for Mexico so the people could enjoy it, not the 30 or 40 families that are billionaires down there.

There are over 24 billionaires in Mexico. The largest amount of billionaires in the world are in Mexico in a country that has nothing. How did they get this money? Legitimately? Did you forget the $100-billion trade deficit we have with dope every year? You do not add that onto the deficit? That is cash. I guess we do not count that. So that just goes into pockets. You do not think all these people are putting all this money into Washington lobbying for all these effects for the benefit of the United States, whether it is Malaysia, China, Korea, Japan. Mexico spent a fortune to lobby for NAFTA.

Who hired some of the best people out of this Congress that retired and out of the Trade Department to represent them? How can you let these people come back here and say that this is what is good for the United States? The United States. What is good for this United States is American jobs. Whether it is 1,000 or 300,000, there never should be a chance for an American to lose his job to anybody.

I want to free trade like Japan. I will trade with anybody. I think Americans can trade. Let me trade with Japan. They are an isolationist country. They have a $60-billion trade deficit with us. Germany. Those are the countries I want to trade with. Italy. England. France. Countries that are not Third World countries. Third World countries. What are we going to sell Malaysia, capital goods to build our products to send back here?

I come from Boston. We had a textile industry and a shoe industry that is all gone and I heard the promises, "Oh, they are going to come back. Do not worry." When is our trade deficit coming back? Where is our surplus coming to? It has not come back since 1973 and this is 24 years. Now we are going to hear the same story, after 38 months, that Mexico and NAFTA is going to be a change down the road? How? What are they going to buy? Those people have no money. There are no consumers. You have to have consumers to buy consumer products. They are buying capital goods to manufacture the products to send here. Then it is going to become a shipping platform, you can believe that, for China, Japan, Germany. They are going to build the products right there. Why? There are no duties. The first thing I would do if I was in Japan, I would say, "Let's build a factory in Mexico so that I can ship it into the United States with no duties." That is the problem.

Do I worry about Mexico? Mexico is not my problem. I am worried about everybody else that is going to go in there, including the multinationals from the United States. I do not worry about Mexico competing against us. I worry about the multinationals and the foreign countries going in there.

It is a disgrace what has happened to this country. Not only there. Believe me, this is just the tip of the iceberg. If you people do not grab hold of the American jobs, I am going to tell you right now, there is going to be an uprising in the inner cities of this country. You have to have jobs—good-paying jobs. That is how you send your kids to school and buy homes. You do not do it on service jobs. I am not going to work at Wal-Mart or I am not going to work at Burger King and I am not going to work at these people that pay $5 an hour. They are nice starter jobs. That is not a job to raise your family on. You have to have manufacturing jobs. And without them, we are dead as a country.

I thank you, Madam Chairman.

[The prepared statement of Mr. DiMare appears in the appendix.]

Ms. ROS-LEHTINEN. Thank you so much.

Mr. DiMare, how would you say that the result of the anti-dumping action that we remember last year was brought to the U.S. International Trade Commission in the finding of dumping against Mexican producers—the Department of Commerce entered into a suspension agreement. I know that you have been very involved with the tomato industry. Do you think that this suspension agreement has been working, or are you satisfied with the way that this case was settled, and do you think that there has been sufficient attention and response given to this problem, specifically in the agricultural area?

Mr. DIMARE. That particular area, in seeing how the stop-gaps in NAFTA were supposed to work, which was supposed to go to the ITC, the International Trade Commission on 201's, we filed twice under 201 in front of the ITC—one being this past year, one being 2 years ago. We lost both times. I am just going through a history of this because I think you should know what has happened with the International Trade Commission. That is a panel of six people, as you know, three Democrats and three Republicans. Supposed to watch over American industry that is hurt by foreign trade. Great watchdog that it is, has ruled twice in favor of American industry. Great job since 1986. Once for Harley-Davidson and once for the corn-growing industry. There have been many cases brought before them. They have never ruled in favor of any of the American industries.

Do you know some of the industries? Tool and die. Said it was not a problem. We have now lost 70 percent of the tool and die industry. Flatware. Said it was not a problem. All the flatware people have gone but Oneida. I mean, these are the case after case after case that has gone in front of them and said there was no problem. "You people do not have any competitive problems with foreign countries."

Ourselves, we lost. They said, "You do not have any problem at all." Since 1991—I will give you some numbers—we were 69 percent. Florida was 69 percent of the total U.S. production of tomatoes. During the winter, we are 95 percent. Mexico was 12.9 percent. In 1995–96, which is just last season—when we finish our season it is usually June—we became 35 percent. We are less than half. Mexico is now 49.5 percent. They are up 400 percent. So, in a 4-year period, we have gone in half and Mexico has increased 400 percent. ITC says, "We cannot see a problem. You people are not shrinking. You do not have a problem whatsoever. Rule against you."

One thing we did get. It was a four-to-one vote, one person abstained. The one person that voted with us, Lynn Bragg, wrote in a statement, published, that this is a total disgrace the way the ITC is handling this case. If this is how they are interpreting the law of the 201, no American company will ever win a 201 case in front of the ITC. This is not what Congress meant. Congress meant aid to companies that are being hurt by imports and we were one of them. We lost.

We filed a dumping case at the same time. Commerce found that, after a long period of time, there were 17 percent margins for dumping against Mexico on tomatoes. During the period of negotiation, they entered into a suspension agreement. If you know anything about suspension agreements, really, the American industry does not have anything to do with it. It is between the American Government and the Mexican growers or Mexican manufacturers, as it would be. And they came to an agreement with a floor price. It is a very minimal price. Our cost is $7.50 to $8 a box to produce tomatoes. The floor price came in at about $5.25. So, as you know, that price certainly is not going to make us any money. We cannot even get our money back. But it did keep suppression of the pressured market. It kept the market from coming to $1 and $2, which it did a lot of times out of Mexico.

It has been working very, very well during the past 3 months. We had one problem this past month during a 3-week period where Mexico shipped in a tremendous volume of product after rains that they had down there and the product was poor. Written into the agreement, there are not supposed to be any prices below the reference price which is 20.68 cents a pound. Commerce has taken it upon themselves, we feel, not to enforce the letter of the law which said that this price would be after all adjustments for quality, backfilling and whatsoever. They have let them adjust these below that price. They have now written a letter saying they do not know where they are. So they got us hung up saying that we have it interpreted your way and a letter to the Mexicans saying, "We really do not agree with you either, so we are both in suspension and do not know what is going to happen. We hope we can have it ratified."

But, along with that and out of the past NAFTA, and I firmly believe this, Congresswoman, I do not think NAFTA could have passed without Florida. And the reason I say this is that the time that you people were trying to pass NAFTA, it was a Democratic president and a Democratic Congress. The Democrats were not for free trade. The Republicans, basically, wanted free trade. And in order to get that, the President—and I have his letter and I am going to put it in the record—from the President of the United States to our Congressman at that time, Tom Lewis, who held out the delegation, except probably for Gibbons, that said they would not vote for NAFTA unless the agricultural industry, the fruit and vegetable industry in Florida, had got some sort of protection to keep them from getting killed. And I want to read it because I think it is very, very important to show that this NAFTA could even have been passed because, I am telling you, Florida was not going to vote for it during that time.

"I know you have been a leader in assuring that under NAFTA our fresh vegetable industry is not adversely affected by unforeseen price changes. I strongly believe that the volume-based snap-back of the existing agreement, coupled with the automatic price monitoring and expedient import relief procedure will be the law after NAFTA is passed. We will provide very effective price and volume discipline. I am committed to take the necessary steps to ensure that USTR and ITC take prompt and effective action to protect the U.S. vegetable industry against price-based import surges from Mexico. I want you to know that I am personally committing to ensuring that this system is enforceable and effective. We will work to ensure against unfair pricing by importers." It is dated November 16, 1993, by Bill Clinton. This was written to get our congressional delegation to vote for NAFTA and we released them, as an industry, against my better judgment, believe it or not, because I did not know about it until afterwards that they had released them. I never released them because I never believed any of the people that we were dealing with at the time. And it has come to prove that.

Ms. ROS-LEHTINEN. Thank you.

Mr. DIMARE. This was done to release them so that you people could get enough votes to pass it. If you tried to pass NAFTA today in Congress, I do not believe you could even get enough votes to get it on the floor. I just believe it is that bad. I do not think any trade agreement today can be passed. People in America are fed up. Talk to the American people. Do not talk to the politicians. Do not talk to these people that are coming up from Commerce and all these people that have these high-falutin' ideas——

Ms. ROS-LEHTINEN. Thank you, Mr. DiMare.

Mr. DIMARE. I am sorry. It just will not be done. It will not pass.

Ms. ROS-LEHTINEN. Thank you. Thank you so much.

Mr. Sherman.

And, by the way, Mr. Carey had to get his flight and he is represented by Mr. William Hamilton, the director of the Department of Government Affairs, and then Mr. Bob Nicklas, who you heard before, of the Legislative Department.

Welcome to both.

Mr. SHERMAN. I would like to thank Mr. DiMare for pointing out that when NAFTA was sold to us, the proponents of NAFTA never hesitated to say so many billion dollars of exports leads to so many jobs. Now that we have a deficit, all of a sudden that becomes phony accounting and you cannot do it that way.

But, aside from my earlier comments here, believe it or not, I am pro-trade and I think we will become a richer country with trade—fair trade, open trade. The problem I have is that invariably every time we figure out a mechanism to increase exports by a billion dollars, the only mechanism that is given to us is entering into an agreement that leads to increasing imports by $2 or $3 or $4 billion. And I like to address my question to Mr. Workman.

Can you give us things we can do to help your members export, leaving aside entering into agreements that will simply open up the most open market in the world even further? What can we do to be more aggressive to help your members export?

Mr. WORKMAN. Well, there are a number of things. But before I get to that, I want to talk a little bit about the trade deficit. And there is no question that it is a problem. But we should look at what is the trade deficit. One-third of the trade deficit is imported oil. Nobody wants to talk about that. That dwarfs the $16-billion trade deficit——

Mr. SHERMAN. But, Mr. Workman, I have a limited amount of time.

Mr. WORKMAN. OK.

Mr. SHERMAN. So I cannot respond to everything you say.

Mr. WORKMAN. What can we do——

Mr. SHERMAN. Mr. Workman—except to point out that when I was growing up, this country was productive enough and rich enough and capable enough in its international trade to run large surpluses that paid for our oil, paid for our foreign aid program, paid for our involvement in the world. And, yes, there are going to be categories where you are not going to grow bananas in Minnesota. We are going to import bananas. We are not going to reach full energy sufficiency. But we once had a country, and we once had a group of international relationships, that allowed us to, on balance, run a surplus. And to say that, "Yes, we would be running a surplus if only we could grow bananas, if only we could find enough oil in the United States so we did not have to import a drop——"

Mr. WORKMAN. Well, I grew up at the same time and in the 1950's, when the United States alone accounted for 50 percent of the industrial output of the world, I would suggest to you that those times will never come again because in the 1950's, you did not have a Germany that challenges us as being the top exporting company in the world. You did not have a Japan. So I think those times are past.

You asked me originally what could you do to help American business, particularly small business, export. I think there are a couple of things that you need to do. One, I think you need to give the executive branch a clear mandate and authority to conduct trade negotiations and I think you ought to keep it, in the immortal words of my chief petty officer in the Navy, "Keep it simple, stupid." Do not clutter it with a lot of non-trade related objectives which are laudable in and of themselves. But, first of all, give them trade negotiating authority.

Second, I think, although we would like it to be, it is not a perfect world. Our competitors' companies have assistance from their governments that we do not have. So the Eximbank, I know it is referred to as corporate welfare in some circles, but we in the business community happen to think that it is a pretty good deal because one of the reasons for it is you cannot get an Eximbank loan unless you can prove you are going to keep jobs in the United States.

Similarly, the Overseas Private Investment Corporation, something that no one ever understands, is actually a good thing for the American taxpayer. The fees are paid for by American companies but they operate in providing political risk insurance in countries that the commercial market will not. Last year, I think they turned back the U.S. Treasury a profit of $208 million. Not a bad deal on the whole for the taxpayer, plus it helps promote exports, it promotes jobs in this country. So those are just a couple of things off the top of my head.

The last thing, I would hope, is that someone here would review the whole concept of imposing unilateral economic sanctions. They do not work. The only people that we hurt are American companies who lose customers, who lose suppliers, and they rarely achieve the purposes that they are intended for. I think we need to rethink this whole concept of unilateral economic sanctions and start over again.

Mr. SHERMAN. If I can just respond for a minute, Mr. Workman, it might surprise you but I believe in this very Committee I spoke out in favor of OPIC and the Eximbank. I do not believe that we should disarm ourselves in the battle for world trade.

You talk about the importance of giving the President fast track, et cetera, and I might be in favor of that if we just added one thing and that was a provision that said that after the agreement was in place, if in any of the first 10 years, on a cumulative basis, we lost out, that we would automatically pull out of that agreement. To give the President the carte blanche to go negotiate something without a guarantee that, as a result of it, either trade would remain on pretty much the same terms or our deficit surplus situation would improve, is asking us to give carte blanche with no guarantee.

And, unfortunately, when the Administration asked us for fast track, they are not going to give us any assurance that the trade agreement where the rubber meets the road—I had to say that because the Teamsters were represented here—is going to lead to an improvement, or at least a neutral situation with our overall trade surplus and deficit.

Madam Chairman, you have been very indulgent.

Ms. ROS-LEHTINEN. Thank you so much.

And Mr. Brady for the final question of the day.

Mr. BRADY. Thank you, Madam Chairwoman. And I am a little puzzled by this note that I received from the Chair that says Mr. DiMare is usually very shy. Please try to draw him out.

Ms. ROS-LEHTINEN. We feed them with strong opinions down in south Florida. It has to be the water.

Mr. BRADY. There are actually two issues I think we agree on. One is the truck safety issue. It is a real concern in America, especially along the border States. Without question, we need more resources to address it and it is interesting that compliance enforcement is almost an assumed part of almost every regulation standard and law that have passed in this country. Except, in this case, it is seen almost as a surprise that we have to apply and reserve and send resources to the States where that truck safety is a real issue. And it is not, in my opinion. It is one that is solvable and does not take away all the other advantages of free trade. But it is one that we have to address immediately.

The second issue we agree on is jobs. It is how we get there that is the issue. Over the last three decades, 80 percent of our new jobs in America have come from exports. Mexico is buying about three dollars out of every ten that is being bought by this country. Ninety-five percent of all the consumers lay outside the American border. Long-term, if we are to find jobs for our constituents, if we are to help trade jobs for union members, it is absolutely essential that we take the steps now that allow cur businesses to be in a position to compete for that trade and to compete means you have to open up your own borders as well.

I guess my point in this whole comment, more than a question, is that long term, if we want to look our children in the eyes and tell them we are taking steps now to allow American companies to compete where the consumers are and where the purchases are for our products to keep our manufacturing base and our informational base and distribution base, we have to—although it is not easy always—take steps like NAFTA to bring that about and this is one of the many steps to do that. But I hope we do not lose sight of the whole overall perspective which is, we do not have a choice if we want to trade jobs long-term for American workers.

Yes, sir.

Mr. HAMILTON. May I respond?

Mr. BRADY. Please.

Mr. HAMILTON. First, President Carey asked me to express his apologies that he could not stay till the end and will certainly be willing to respond in writing if there is anything you specifically need.

But this notion of cross-border freight shipment is not brand new. We have had trade with Mexico long before we had NAFTA and we have always been able to handle that in a fairly intelligent way and that is, historically, Mexican freight coming into this country has been dropped at the border. American trucks have then picked it up and carried it to its destination. Conversely, export traffic into Mexico has been handled the same way. We have dropped it at the border. The Mexican companies have picked it up and taken it. There is nothing new here.

Now, there are ways you can fix or try to fix the enforcement problem at the border. California has just spent $28 million for new inspection facilities. It is a beginning. But it is a drop in the bucket. As a Texan like yourself, I am ashamed to say that Texas has not done much in that direction. Our situation in Laredo is pitiful. In El Paso, it is not much better. Del Rio is a joke.

Texas can spend a lot of money—its money or the Federal Government's money—to build up its enforcement mechanism and maybe, instead of stopping one out of 200 trucks for inspection, maybe we will stop five out of 200, or ten out of 200. And maybe we will catch 20 percent of the drugs and 50 percent of the hazardous materials over the next 50 years or so.

But there is a much cheaper, simpler way to handle that problem. Not the larger problem. Not the overall trade deficit problem. But the trucking problem can be solved by simply amending the agreement to ensure that materials coming into this country from Mexico are handled by Americans once they get into this country and that materials going out of this country into Mexico are handled by Mexicans. It is pretty simple. Pretty straightforward. Pretty cheap. And I would commend the Committee to take a hard look at that possibility and see if, particularly since the President seems to want to extend the madness and have a new fast track authority and have an extended NAFTA, then maybe as part of the bargain Congress requires him to do that.

Mr. BRADY. Mr. Workman, your comments?

Mr. WORKMAN. That is an interesting concept. It assumes that we can unilaterally amend a contract that we signed with two other parties. And, as an old trade negotiator, I am curious as to why would the Mexicans and the Canadians want to agree to go back to basically where they were in 1992?

Mr. BRADY. And I did not intend to start a free-for-all here at the panel, Madam Chairwoman. But I appreciate the comments from both people.

Mr. HAMILTON. Well, do you want me to respond, since he raised the question?

Ms. ROS-LEHTINEN. One minute?

Mr. HAMILTON. Sure.

Ms. ROS-LEHTINEN. Thank you.

Mr. HAMILTON. The Mexican trucking industry is against the current arrangement. The Mexican trucking companies are against the arrangement that was negotiated. Frankly, as an organization that lives and exists to negotiate agreements, I find it baffling that the Bush Administration would have negotiated such a sorry deal or that the Clinton Administration would have bought into it. And there is nothing wrong with admitting that we made a mistake and backing up and trying to fix it. I think significant elements of the Mexican people would support that. The overwhelming majority of the American people would.

Ms. ROS-LEHTINEN. Thank you so much. Thank you to all three panelists for giving wonderful testimony. We will have some other Members who might submit questions for the record and if you could respond to them, we would appreciate it. Thank you.

The Subcommittee is now adjourned.

[Whereupon, at 4:32 p.m., the Subcommittee was adjourned.]

APPENDIX

AMO HOUGHTON
31ST DISTRICT, NEW YORK

MEMBER:
NORTHEAST-MIDWEST
COALITION

COMMITTEES:
COMMITTEE ON WAYS
AND MEANS
SUBCOMMITTEE ON TRADE
SUBCOMMITTEE ON HEALTH

COMMITTEE ON
INTERNATIONAL RELATIONS
SUBCOMMITTEE ON AFRICA

Congress of the United States
House of Representatives

Congressman Amo Houghton (NY-31)
Testimony on the North American Free Trade Agreement
Subcommittee on International Economic Policy and Trade
2172 Rayburn House Office Building
March 5, 1997

Madame Chair, thank you so much for inviting me to appear before your subcommittee to talk about NAFTA. As a former businessman and currently a member of the Ways and Means Subcommittee on Trade, I'm clearly interested in NAFTA and its effect on the U.S. economy and jobs -- particularly the economy and jobs in the 31st District of New York.

Let me start by saying that it is not unimportant that we get the facts straight about NAFTA. NAFTA *is* working. It breaks down Mexican trade barriers and boosts U.S. exports. When the economy surges, NAFTA spurs U.S. export growth and creates jobs here in the U.S. When the economy slows down, NAFTA limits our export losses and preserves U.S. jobs.

Before NAFTA, Mexican tariffs on U.S. exports averaged 2 1/2 times more than U.S. tariffs on Mexican exports. Already -- and keep in mind that it has only been three years -- the average Mexican tariff on U.S. products has dropped more than 50%. In 1994, NAFTA's first year of operation, U.S. exports surged over

1110 LONGWORTH HOUSE OFFICE BUILDING
WASHINGTON, DC 20515-3231
PHONE: (202) 225-3161
FAX: (202) 225-6574

32 DENISON PARKWAY WEST
CORNING, NY 14830
(607) 937-3333
1-(800) 562-7431

FEDERAL BUILDING, ROOM 122
JAMESTOWN, NY 14701
(716) 484-0252

700 WESTGATE PLAZA
OLEAN, NY 14760
(716) 372-2127

268 GENESEE ST.
AUBURN, NY 13021
1-(800) 562-7431

22%, from $41.5 billion to $50.7 billion. Despite Mexico's economic problems and peso gyrations which dropped U.S. exports, the U.S. still sent $46.3 billion worth of goods to Mexico in 1995. Last year, U.S. exports to Mexico rebounded to a record level -- $56.2 billion -- an increase of over 21% since 1995. Exports to Canada rose more than 33% of the pre-NAFTA level.

You see, NAFTA has created fair rules for trade with Mexico. NAFTA "locks in" Mexico's lowered barriers to U.S. exports, acting as a safety net by ensuring that Mexico continues to favor U.S. exports. For instance, when the Mexican government raised tariffs on 4,500 products in 1995 because of its economic problems, NAFTA forced it to exempt the goods coming in from the U.S..

This increase in export activity and decrease in tariff barriers means to people in the United States one thing: creation of jobs -- better jobs -- for Americans. The United States Trade Representative reports that over 11 million U.S. jobs depend on exports -- that's up 1.5 million from four years ago. It's been said that jobs directly supported by exported goods pay around 15% more than the average U.S. job. That's good news for the American worker.

There are some who accuse NAFTA for being responsible for lost jobs despite the fact that jobs move back and forth according to corporate conditions or directions. In general, these accusations are not based on logic. For instance, some look to certifications for the NAFTA Transitional Adjustment Assistance program (NAFTA-TAA). It is not accurate to say that these jobs have been lost solely due to NAFTA. NAFTA-TAA certifications say nothing about jobs being lost "because of" NAFTA. The Labor Department has not certified any job losses as being "due to NAFTA."

One example is the case of Mattel. Some Mattel employees who lost jobs were certified under NAFTA-TAA even though NAFTA could not have been a cause of their job loss, since U.S. tariffs on toys from Mexico were **zero** even before NAFTA went into place. As I said, there is no requirement under NAFTA-TAA to show that the Agreement itself caused job loss. Employees need to show only that imports from Mexico and Canada were one factor behind job loss, or that some of the employers' production was shifted to either country. Imports from our neighbors and production shifts would occur with or without NAFTA, and people can qualify for NAFTA-TAA benefits even if factors besides imports or production shifts were the real cause of job loss, such as corporate restructuring or new technology.

I also take issue with several NAFTA opponents who say that every $1 billion of imports from Mexico costs the U.S. 20,000 jobs. They arrive at this conclusion based on a Commerce Department estimate that on average, every $1 billion of total U.S. exports supports 20,000 U.S. jobs. This number primarily reflects the jobs companies need to add to meet export demand. There is hardly proof that this export-based estimate has anything to do with imports. It is wrong to assume that a company competing with imports inevitably shuts down production. Companies can compete effectively for the domestic market, and certainly can continue to export. I know this personally.

Having said all of this, Madame Chair, it is important to note that the full benefits of NAFTA will not be apparent for several years. As you know, NAFTA has been in effect for only three years. Many reductions in Mexican trade barriers are being phased in over five to fifteen years. The Mexican government is taking actions needed to stabilize its economy, and in some cases is actually speeding up meeting NAFTA commitments to open its markets.

I have to believe that NAFTA is extremely important to the United States. Canada and Mexico are our first and third largest trading partners. We entered NAFTA because of the need to expand trade, to create jobs, to raise our standard of living, and to remain competitive in an increasingly competitive world. NAFTA is helping us accomplish those goals. We are now hoping to bring Chile into NAFTA. I visited Chile with a group of businessmen from the 31st District last year. It is my opinion, and not incidentally the opinion of the business leaders with me on the trade mission, that Chile's accession to NAFTA is essential, and should happen soon.

Madame Chair, let me close by saying that after three years, it is apparent to me that NAFTA is the key to opening markets and expanding our economy in conjunction with the two countries who are not only two of our largest three trading partners, but who share our borders.

Thank you for allowing me to testify today.

Testimony by Ambassador Ira Shapiro
before the
Subcommittee on International Economic Policy and Trade
of the
House International Relations Committee
March 5, 1997

Introduction

Madame Chairman, thank you for inviting me to appear today before the Subcommittee on International Economic Policy and Trade to discuss the North American Free Trade Agreement (NAFTA). I welcome the opportunity to address the NAFTA as an issue with this Subcommittee and the Congress.

I think we can all agree that the results of U.S. economic policy, including trade policy, are a bedrock issue of importance for the American people, the President and his Administration and the Congress. The President's commitment is unwavering to a trade policy that holds of central the importance the opening of foreign markets and breaking down of trade barriers as part of the Administration's economic strategy. The United States, through the best tradition of bipartisan cooperation in Congress and Executive Branch leadership, has done more to open markets in the last four years than at any time in history. There is no doubt that global markets are now more open to U.S. goods and services than was the case four years ago. Make no mistake, this tradition of bipartisan cooperation and Executive Branch leadership is now more important than ever to our economic prosperity both now and in the future.

The American economy as you know, is now in its sixth year of economic expansion with good prospects for continued growth. More than 11 million new jobs have been added to the economy since January 1993, and we have had the lowest combined rates of unemployment and inflation since the 1960s. The U.S. economy is clearly a high achiever in the global context. Not surprisingly, it has been determined to be the most competitive economy in the world for the last few years by prestigious independent experts. We have very little to fear in the global economy and have much to gain.

The importance of trade in our domestic economy today is profound. In 1970, the value of two-way trade equaled 13% of U.S. GDP. In 1996, trade was nearly 30% of GDP, or about $2.3 trillion. More than eleven million U.S. jobs now depend on exports -- 1.5 million more than just four years ago. Jobs supported by goods exports wages are 13-16% higher than non trade-related jobs in the economy. Over the last four years, roughly one quarter of our economic growth has come from exports. In the last four years, U.S. manufactured exports are up 42 percent, high technology exports are up 45 percent, services exports are up 26 percent and agricultural exports are up 40 percent.

To best grasp the importance of trade policy, however, one simply needs to recognize that over 95 percent of the world's consumers reside outside the United States. Our prosperity literally depends upon our ability to effectively tap into this huge opportunity, particularly the emerging markets of the world that are the fastest growing and largest. For example, the Western Hemisphere and the Asian Pacific Rim now account for nearly 70 percent of total U.S. exports, up from 65 percent just four years ago. Both the Asian Pacific Rim and Latin America are the fastest growing markets in the world. Latin America alone, if current trends continue, will exceed both Japan and Western Europe combined as an export market for U.S. goods by the year 2010.

American economic success is a tribute to our companies and our workers, who are clearly demonstrating they are the most competitive in the world. For that reason, the trade policy of this Administration has relentlessly pursued market openings abroad -- multilaterally wherever possible, regionally when appropriate, and bilaterally when necessary. We should welcome reciprocal trade agreements that break down barriers to trade because of our proven ability to compete. Even more, we should aggressively seek such agreements because our economy is still far more open than that of our trading partners. As a result, trade agreements create a more level playing field for our producers and exporters.

The NAFTA in U.S. Trade Policy

The NAFTA has been a key component of our trade policy. It is creating a new competitive environment in North America that is fairer and driven more by market forces rather than barriers to commerce. Particularly as it pertains to U.S. - Mexico trade relations, this transformation should not be underestimated for its importance to a vibrant commercial relationship. We knew before we entered into the NAFTA that Mexico would have to make much greater changes to its trade and economic regime, and this has proven to be the case:

- Mexico's average tariffs were 10 percent, versus 4 percent for the United States;
- Mexico had substantial local content and export requirements, quotas and trade balancing rules where the U.S. had few barriers of this type;
- Mexico had a weak intellectual property regime;
- Mexico's services, and financial services, market was closed in many respects;
- Mexico's government procurement regime was largely closed to foreign producers and service providers;
- Mexico's technical standards for goods and services was not disciplined by the rigors of a strong set of rules in this area;
- Mexico's sanitary and phytosanitary regime for agricultural products lacked the framework of clear rules premised on sound science; and
- Mexico's telecommunications services market was largely closed.

The creation of NAFTA. the world's largest free trade area, was unprecedented in its scale and complexity. We are still some years away from full implementation of the agreement, and therefore full evaluation of its impact. However, the NAFTA is a success and is working to promote and benefit the interests of U.S. workers and firms.

NAFTA has played a vital role in helping trade expansion strengthen the U.S. economy. Nevertheless, it is not a simple matter to measure the impact of the agreement, for two major reasons. First, Mexico's economy is less than 1/20th the size of our own, so any impact will be relatively small on our very large economy. Second, NAFTA's provisions are being phased in over transitions periods up to 15 years long. Reviewing the Agreement after only 3 years means many of the changes required by the NAFTA are still far from full implementation and are not yet affecting trade and investment decisions. As you know, a report from the President on the impact of the NAFTA on the U.S. economy is something the Administration is now developing and will be providing by July as required by the NAFTA implementing legislation.

Nevertheless, we do have data that provides a basis for our assessment that the NAFTA has been working to promote the interests of the United States. Simply put, trade agreements are intended to open opportunities for increased trade flows. This measure of success - an increase in business - is also how many firms measure their own success. NAFTA's results here are unambiguous. U.S. goods exports to both Mexico and Canada set records last year; exports to Canada were $134 billion -- which is 33 percent above 1993 levels, while those to Mexico were $57 billion -- 37 percent above 1993 levels.

Another traditional measure is market share -- many businesses measure their success by their increase in their share of total sales. Again, our trade with Mexico is a clear success by this measure. In 1993, our share of Mexico's total imports was 69 percent. This has increased each year since NAFTA, to 76 percent through June of 1996.

Our economy today is the envy of the world: for its job creation, for its low inflation, for the enormous surge in investment, and for its strength across the board. We lead the world in aircraft and agriculture. We set the pace in software and computers and telecommunications -- the products of the global information highway. We have surged back strongly in sectors that were hard hit five or tens years ago -- autos, auto parts, machine tools, steel, semiconductors, etc.

Our industrial production is up 18 percent in four years. We are expanding industrial capacity at the fastest rate since the 1970s. We have gained 185,000 manufacturing jobs over the past four years, despite strong U.S. manufacturing productivity growth. The average U.S. manufacturing worker produced 13 percent more per hour worked in 1996 than in 1992. Our performance has been very strong in almost every region of the nation, but the resurgence has been particularly strong in the heartland, in the industrial Midwest, where there has been a virtual renaissance of production and manufacturing. Trade and exports have played a critical part in that resurgence.

As we assess NAFTA today, I would acknowledge that exports to Mexico did not grow as rapidly in the first two years as we had hoped, because of the depth of the peso crisis and the Mexican recession. We are gratified, however, by the strong recovery of exports in 1996.

But fair minded observers should acknowledge that the fears of the NAFTA critics have not materialized. There is certainly no evidence of significant job loss owing to the NAFTA, in an economy that has been strong enough across the board that we have created 8.5 million new jobs in three years. There has certainly been no loss of investment from the U.S. and Mexico since the NAFTA. In 1995, the latest data available, the total foreign investment into Mexico, from all sources, was less than $7 billion. In contrast, total foreign direct investment into the U.S. was over $60 billion, and total gross private domestic investment in the U.S. last year was over $1.1 trillion, nearly three quarters of which was business investment. It turns out that the U.S. is both the world's leading generator of, and magnet for, investment, which calls into question the NAFTA critics' basic premise that investment would move wholesale into low wage countries.

Rather, the evidence shows that the NAFTA has contributed to the strength of our economy. I had occasion last July to speak in Chicago along with Governor Jim Edgar of Illinois. At that time, he said that today's event -- the completion of production of the largest machine tool ever built in North America -- demonstrates:

"The North American Free Trade Agreement is working for the benefit of Illinois workers and their families. In the first two years after it was ratified, the NAFTA has helped to create and sustain nearly 30,000 new jobs in Illinois. Today, more than 150,000 Illinois residents are working because of exports through the NAFTA. Whatever language you speak -- English, Spanish, whatever -- the NAFTA translates into jobs."

The NAFTA's Value in the Difficult Economic Times

In evaluating the NAFTA, we must also keep in mind that we can't directly compare the two relevant situations: the world with NAFTA and the world without NAFTA. We have to make to intelligent guesses about what a world without NAFTA would look like. And we also have to consider what negative outcomes the NAFTA may have prevented.

The NAFTA serves as a buffer against reduced access to the Mexican and Canadian economies -- without which access to more than 120 million consumers would be jeopardized and more than two million high-wage U.S. jobs would be put at risk. Let me underscore this point. NAFTA, in the case of Mexico, has been responsible for preventing economic harm as well as promoting economic gain.

Specifically, NAFTA did not cause the peso crisis in late 1994 and early 1995, nor the related 1995 Mexican recession and the decline in U.S. goods exports. Decisions made by the Mexican government on exchange-rate policy in the 1980s, combined with developments in 1994 in financial markets in and outside Mexico led to the peso crisis. However, during this period, the NAFTA was extremely important in protecting U.S. export-supported jobs and U.S. economic interests. Because of the NAFTA, U.S. goods exports fared much better in 1995 than after the last Mexican financial crisis in 1982.

During that earlier crisis, before Mexico's adherence to either the GATT or the NAFTA, government officials were free to take arbitrary measures to restrict entry of imports. They imposed 100 percent duties on American products and strict licensing requirements, moves that caused U.S. goods exports to plunge by 50 percent between 1981 and 1983. U.S. jobs supported by goods exports to Mexico were cut by more than half, from an estimated 431,000 in 1981 to 201,000 in 1983. It took nearly seven years for U.S. exports to Mexico to return to their level of 1981.

The situation in 1995 was very different. Instead of putting up barriers to U.S. exports, Mexico continued to reduce barriers as the NAFTA requires. This is no small accomplishment in the midst of what was a very deep economic contraction. By contrast, Mexico did place additional restrictions on imports from its non-FTA trade partners. While the U.S. share of Mexico's goods imports rose in 1994 and 1995, imports from Western Europe, Japan and Korea fell by 25.5 percent, 24.5 percent and 64 percent, respectively.

As the Mexican economy begins to stabilize and grow again, there has been a strong recovery of U.S. exports. In 1996, U.S. goods exports to Mexico were nearly 23 percent higher than in 1995. In other words, it only took 18 months for U.S. exports to Mexico to fully recover from the December 1994 peso crisis, not the 7 years needed after the 1982 peso crisis.

Understandably, concern has been expressed about the significant swing in the bilateral goods trade balance, from U.S. surplus of $1.3 billion in 1994 to a deficit $15.4 billion in 1995. However, the fact is that the trade deficit arose largely from Mexico's peso crisis and the resulting recession, not NAFTA.

In 1995 Mexico experienced its worst economic downturn in modern history in 1995. Production fell by nearly 7 percent, making Mexico's recession about three times worse than the last U.S. recession in 1991-1992. Mexico's imports fell and the sharp decline in its domestic spending power made more of its remaining production available for export.

In essence, the trade balance shifted because of a Mexican recession that reduced Mexican employment by 1.6 million and substantially reduced incomes and domestic demand. At the same time, the United States was in its fourth year of economic expansion; U.S. jobs expanded by 1.7 million; and real national income by 2.5 percent. The shift in the bilateral goods trade balance in 1995 did not come at the expense of our workers.

The NAFTA will continue to serve the interests of the U.S. economy and U.S. workers long after the current Mexican recession is a distant memory. NAFTA's existence has not only kept Mexico on track toward more open markets for U.S. exports, it has supported Mexican government efforts to sustain the course of internal economic reform and thereby minimized any negative repercussions of the peso crisis and the economic downturn on U.S. workers. Mexico has made major efforts in recent years to pursue economic policies more similar to those of the United States. In contrast to 1981 when Mexico was a closed economy, the more open Mexican economy of today is much better positioned to recover rapidly from its problems in 1995. Growth in Mexico was estimated to have exceeded 5 percent in 1996, and is forecast to stay strong beyond 1996. An open, rapidly growing Mexican economy will help the United States.

The overwhelming and growing share of Mexico's imports come from the United States.

NAFTA and U.S. Workers

Ultimately, the reasons the United States entered the NAFTA with Mexico are for the benefits to U.S. workers. NAFTA greatly expands the opportunities of U.S. export industries in Mexico and thus for the expansion of higher wage jobs in the United States. Our export industries are among our most productive and dynamic of all U.S. industries. The jobs they support pay wages that are 13 percent to 16 percent higher than the U.S. national average wage and these jobs tend to be more secure.

We do have good estimates of jobs supported by exports because of the knowledge we have about how exports actually are produced in the U.S. economy. We estimate the increase in U.S. jobs supported by exports to Canada and Mexico since the first day of NAFTA implementation at 311,000. However, we have less knowledge about the jobs displaced by imports because of the variable effect of imports on domestic production. Some imports are complements to domestic production. Some imports are products we not produce, or are in short supply. Some do displace domestic production. One thing is clear: It is not accurate to utilize the methodology the Administration uses to estimate the jobs supported by exports to estimate the job displacement impact of imports. The methodology is simply not designed to address the import displacement impact since the variables are different.

Those citing estimates of the jobs displaced by imports with our NAFTA partners also often use the number of workers certified for training assistance provided by the NAFTA Trade Adjustment Assistance (TAA) program administered by the Department of Labor. Through February 24, 1997, about 110,408 U.S. workers were certified as eligible. It is important to put this figure in context:

- The U.S. economy is currently creating this number of jobs in about two weeks; net employment has increased by 8.9 million during this period.

- Workers that may have been displaced by imports from NAFTA countries in general, or Mexico in particular, made up less than 1 percent of total estimated involuntary job displacement in the U.S. over this period.

In short, the adjustment being caused by trade with Mexico and Canada is much less significant than that due to the changes in our own evolving economy, and in fact comes at a time when we have created jobs and opportunities at a rapid rate. Furthermore, the NAFTA TAA program provides the best such adjustment assistance available to workers who meet the criteria of the program, and this is the case even when the NAFTA provisions were not responsible for the job loss or dislocation. The only consideration in this instance is whether imports increased or production was relocated, even, for instance, if the tariff rate in the U.S. was zero before the NAFTA went into effect.

Labor Standards and Environmental Protection

I would like to turn briefly to some of the broader issues that are raised by NAFTA, specifically, labor standards and the environment. In both these instances, the United States is breaking new ground by working with our North American neighbors on the use of cooperative, multilateral institutions to address transnational issues of concern. In negotiating the NAFTA, this Administration concluded an unprecedented series of agreements designed to help ensure that expanded trade does not take place at the expense of the protection of worker rights or the environment. And despite the fact that these agreements have only been in place for three years, they are already yielding concrete results.

Labor

The North American Agreement on Labor Cooperation (NAALC) is an innovative approach attempting to ensure high levels of worker rights protection. Two premises make up the foundation of the NAALC: 1) The Agreement commits the Parties to eleven labor principles, ranging from freedom of association to the protection of migrant workers; and 2) the Agreement affirms respect for the Parties' sovereignty and their labor laws and commits the Parties to the enforcement of those laws.

The objectives of the NAALC include: improving working conditions and living standards in each party's territory; promoting basic labor law principles; encouraging cooperation to promote innovation and rising levels of productivity and quality; pursuing cooperative labor-related activities; and promoting compliance with, and effective enforcement by each party of, its "labor law" and fostering transparency in the administration of labor laws. Under the agreement, citizens of any NAFTA signatory can request their government to review labor practices in one of its NAFTA partners. Review results are made public. Governments also may request consultations at the Cabinet level and a detailed examination of any incident or labor practice in another NAFTA country.

In our view, important freedom of association issues that have been raised in the submissions process are now being addressed to a greater degree within Mexico and continue to be the subject of serious ongoing debate within that country. For example:

- The Mexican Supreme Court has found that state laws that restrict union organization in the state governments are unconstitutional. The types of restrictions addressed in the decision had been reviewed and publicly reported on by the U.S. National Administrative Office (NAO) in the submission process.

- Issues of union registration and internal union democracy were an important component of the six submissions reviewed by the U.S. NAO. In August, 1996, the Secretary of Labor of Mexico, together with the major labor and business organization, signed a document in the Presidential Palace, in the presence of President Zedillo, committing their respective organizations to addressing these matters, among others.

Over the past three years, in addition to the submission process that is in part designed to bring important issues to the attention of decision makers, an extensive program of trinational cooperative activities has been under taken by the National Administrative Offices of Canada, Mexico and the U.S. Some examples of these activities are:

- trinational study tours to exchange best practices to reduce worker fatalities and injuries;
- seminars and conferences on labor law and worker rights; and
- a conference this year on "Child and Youth Labor in North America," which will examine innovations that seek to eliminate illegal child labor and improve workplace conditions for legally employed children.

The impact of the NAALC can only be measured in the long term. Quantifiable and objectively verifiable indicators of progress in the area of labor rights and standards are difficult under any circumstances. However, we have reliable and consistent information that Mexico's government as well as labor and business institutions are keenly aware of the scrutiny underway by the NAALC institutions as regards such areas as freedom of association and the right to organize and bargain collectively. Furthermore, the cooperative undertakings that have been initiated are also important in encouraging appropriate respect for the rights of the workers as well as their welfare in all respects. These are important facts that should not be underestimated for their value.

Environment

The NAFTA and its associated agreements created new institutions designed to address environmental concerns, not only in the U.S.-Mexico border region, but across the North American continent. These institutions are sponsoring cooperative activities to address an impressive range of environmental issues.

For instance, in a combined effort to address long-standing environmental infrastructure problems along the U.S.-Mexico border, the United States and Mexico created the Border Environment Cooperation Commission (BECC) and the North American Development Bank (NADBank). Since their establishment in 1995, the BECC has certified twelve environmental infrastructure projects and has nearly 100 additional projects in the pipeline. To date, the NADBank has approved financing for four of these projects. These projects are primarily wastewater treatment plants, which once constructed, will significantly reduce pollution in the U.S.-Mexico border area. Completion of these projects will result in significantly reducing environmental problems in such locations as: Mercedes, Texas; Brawley and Somerton, California; and numerous towns on the Mexican side of the border.

The importance of these kinds of infrastructure projects for addressing environmental problems in the border region should not be underestimated. For instance, the International Boundary and Water Commission (IBWC), which is working closely with the BECC and other NAFTA institutions, recently completed construction of a $56 million international wastewater treatment system at Nuevo Laredo, and is near completion of the primary treatment plant for the $250 million international wastewater treatment system in San Diego/Tijuana. The Nuevo Laredo system already in test operation, will effectively remove the most serious pollution from the entire Rio Grande. The San Diego facility, which will begin interim operation in April 1997, will -- for the first time in 50 years -- provide a permanent solution to the Tijuana sewage problem, resulting in a clean Tijuana estuary, and clean U.S. and Mexican beaches in the San Diego/Tijuana area.

Moreover, the environmental benefits of NAFTA are not limited to the U.S.-Mexico border area. The Commission for Environmental Cooperation (CEC), which was created under the North American Agreement on Environmental Cooperation (NAAEC), is promoting increased cooperation among the three NAFTA parties to protect and conserve the North American environment. In the first two years of operation, the CEC has begun work on an impressive list of environmental projects. For instance, the three NAFTA countries have created an Environmental Enforcement and Compliance Cooperation working group to discuss areas of collaborative enforcement efforts, including such issues as transboundary hazardous waste tracking, and wildlife and CFC smuggling. Moreover, the CEC process by which citizens may request an investigation of inadequate enforcement of a country's environmental laws, is working well. The Secretariat has handled the six submissions it has received to date carefully and responsibly. It is interesting to note that, of these submissions, only one concerns Mexico.

The deplorable environmental problems that currently exist in the U.S.-Mexico border region were decades in the making, and we cannot expect to correct them overnight. However, the environmental institutions created by NAFTA are providing us with powerful tools to begin to address these problems. This Administration remains committed to working with our NAFTA partners to address the environmental problems, not only in the U.S.-Mexico border region, but across the North American continent.

Conclusion

The Administration recognizes that the NAFTA implementing legislation was approved by Congress and signed by the President after a bitter struggle. The hearing today reminds us that this issue is still controversial. However, now three years after that struggle the Administration is certain it was the right decision.

No one can dispute that fact that the NAFTA is opening the Mexican market - our third largest export market with far more room to grow - to a far greater degree. The Mexican economic reform process is also in good part locked in by the comprehensive rules of the NAFTA and the agreement is an important encouragement to yet more market based reforms.

We have launched an unprecedented effort with Mexico to address labor and environmental considerations that goes beyond anything the United States has done with any other developing country, and it is starting to show results.

The NAFTA serves as our most important step to date towards the Administration's commitment to free and fair trade in the Americas. This hemisphere includes the fastest growing market for

U.S. exports, that being Latin America.

Madame Chairman, now is the time to continue to chart the important course that builds on our strength and openness to ensure that we open markets around the world and fight for fairness in the global trading arena. I will be happy to take questions.

Testimony of Regina K. Vargo
Deputy Assistant Secretary for the Western Hemisphere
U.S. Department of Commerce
before the
Subcommittee on International Economic Policy and Trade
of the
House International Relations Committee
March 5, 1997

Madame Chairman, thank you for the opportunity to appear today before the Subcommittee on International Economic Policy and Trade to discuss the impact of the North American Free Trade Agreement (NAFTA) on U.S. trade.

Introduction

The NAFTA trade relationship is our largest in the world. Our NAFTA partners buy $3 out of every $10 that the United States exports. They also supply $3 out of every $10 that the United States purchases from other countries.

In 1996, U.S. trade within NAFTA stood at $420 billion. While Canada and Mexico have long been our first and third largest trading partners, almost one-third of current trade levels is new trade that has taken place in the three years since NAFTA was implemented. To put this tremendous increase in trade in perspective, if the $127 billion trade gain under NAFTA were a separate country, it would be our fourth largest trading partner.

We have now completed our third year under the North American Free Trade Agreement (NAFTA). While the Administration has not completed its comprehensive study of how NAFTA has affected the U.S. economy (due to the Congress by July 1, 1997, as part of NAFTA's implementing legislation), we can say that NAFTA has met the Administration's objectives of expanding and protecting U.S. exports to Mexico and Canada. In fact, in 1996, U.S. exports of $190 billion to Canada and Mexico were larger than our exports to any other area of the world, including the entire Pacific Rim or all of Europe.

Increased market access for U.S. products was a key Administration objective under NAFTA. While NAFTA phases out tariffs and trade barriers over 15 years, most of the trade within North America is already duty-free. This is the last year of dutiable trade between the United States and Canada. In January 1998, the last tariffs between our two countries will be eliminated, under the terms of the U.S.-Canada Free Trade Agreement which were incorporated into the NAFTA. In the case of Mexico, four rounds of tariff cuts have reduced the tariff discrepancy between the United States and Mexico. A rough estimate suggests that Mexican tariffs, which had averaged 10 percent before NAFTA, now average less than 6 percent, while average U.S. tariffs have fallen from 4 percent to about 2.5 percent. These tariff preferences are only available for goods made in North America; tough rules of origin determine whether a good qualifies and reward companies using North American parts and labor. As the duties are phased out, the incentive to use North American goods increases.

Tariff reductions tell only part of the story, however. One of the clearest examples of how non-tariff barriers can limit U.S. market access is in the automotive sector. Under the former Mexican Auto Regime, U.S. companies were required to produce in Mexico in order to sell there. Local content requirements and trade balancing requirements were so severe that virtually all vehicles sold in Mexico were produced locally with mostly Mexican parts -- the United States was able to export only 4,000 cars and 2,000 trucks annually to Mexico under the old rules, even though Mexico was considered to be one of the fastest growing automotive markets in the world. The Administration estimated that removing these restrictions would open up $1 billion in new export opportunities for U.S. companies. While NAFTA is phasing out Mexico's automotive restrictions over a ten-year period, U.S. auto companies have already realized these gains. In 1996, the United States exported 51,000 new passenger cars and 31,500 new trucks to Mexico, for a value of $1 2 billion. Without NAFTA, automotive trade would be a one-way street heading north.

Mexico

A second major U.S. objective for NAFTA was to "lock-in" the trade liberalization and economic reforms which the Government of Mexico had undertaken unilaterally in the years before the Agreement. These reforms had prompted a three-fold increase in U.S. exports to Mexico in the period of 1986-1993, yet were subject to change in Mexican policy. The importance of these commitments became apparent during the peso crisis of December 1994 and the ensuing Mexican recession, the Mexican response to which was sharply different than to a devaluation of similar magnitude in 1982.

In the earlier crisis, Mexico acted to restore balance to its international accounts by restricting imports. Mexico raised tariffs to 100 percent and imposed import licensing requirements on all products. It also acted to exert much more government control over the market by nationalizing large segments of the economy. The result was a 50 percent drop in U.S. exports, which took nearly seven years to recover as the Mexican economy stagnated and Mexican imports were tightly controlled.

In contrast, U.S. exports to Mexico fell by only 9 percent in the year following the 1994 peso devaluation, despite the fact that real Mexican GDP fell 7 percent. And the recovery of the Mexican economy has been much quicker and sharper than most observers forecasted. With the return of Mexican economic growth (5.1 percent) in 1996, U.S. exports surpassed their pre-NAFTA peak by $15 billion to reach a record $57 billion. Moreover, there are indications that this export growth is accelerating (Chart 1). By the fourth quarter of 1996, U.S. exports to Mexico were growing at an annualized rate of $64 billion, compared to $52 billion earlier in the year. This is directly related to growth in Mexico (Chart 2). As Mexico's economy grows, it will consume more of what it is now exporting and demand for U.S. products will increase. If the trends of late 1996 continue into 1997, we can expect to see the merchandise trade deficit, which was $16 billion in 1996, narrow this year.

While U.S. export sales to Mexico in recent years have been strongly impacted by macro economic conditions, important elements of this trade clearly would not have taken place without NAFTA. For one thing, as Mexico kept its market open to U.S. exports and met its NAFTA requirements to further lower tariffs, the U.S. market share in Mexico grew from 69 percent in 1993 to 76 percent in 1996, a gain which should position U.S. exporters well as the Mexican economy continues its recovery. In addition, NAFTA has encouraged steadfastness in Mexico's economic reforms. The Zedillo Administration has continued to move forward with privatization or concessions of important sectors of the economy, such as railroads, seaports and airports. Greater competition has been encouraged in telecommunications, natural gas distribution and financial markets.

Responding to the above, U.S. exports to Mexico of industrial goods exceeded $16.5 billion last year, a 21 percent increase over 1995. Similarly, U.S. exports of capital goods increased 17 percent to over $18 billion. More recently, there are signs of resumed consumer activity in Mexico. It is interesting to note that in contrast to 1996, when exports formed the basis of the Mexican recovery, the Zedillo Administration forecasts that roughly half of 1997's

44-878 98 - 3

forecasted growth of 4 percent will come from a pickup in domestic consumption, as Mexican employment levels and real wages rise.

Certainly, some of the U.S. export sales are related to Mexico's success in "exporting its way" out of its current account problems. Coproduction between U.S. and Mexican companies continues to be an important feature of U.S. purchases from Mexico, and strengthens U.S. competitiveness in our own market and overseas. In addition, with the collapse of its internal market in 1995, Mexican industry sought new markets for its products, and NAFTA provided Mexican products that could claim NAFTA preferences and origin with a competitive edge in the U.S. market. The extent to which imports from Mexico are substituting for imports from other sources is one of the issues we will be examining in the NAFTA Study due in July. Like our exports, U.S. imports from Mexico also set a new record in 1996, reaching $73 billion. Mexico's ability to sell its products overseas enabled it to weather the economic crisis and pay back three years early its debt to the United States that it incurred as part of the President's support program for the peso.

Canada

Trade with Canada, our largest trading partner, is growing too. With $290 billion in two-way merchandise trade taking place in 1996, the U.S.-Canada relationship is the largest in the world. U.S. exports to Canada in 1996 were $134 billion, while imports totaled $157 billion. The macroeconomic situation in Canada also had an impact on trade flows last year. The Canadian economy in 1996 was marked by relatively low growth (1.5%) and a high unemployment rate (10%). The falling Canadian dollar has also depressed demand for U.S. products. U.S. exports grew just over 5 percent in 1996, as opposed to nearly 11 percent in

1995. However, there are signs of economic improvement in Canada, and the Bank of Canada forecasts the Canadian economy to grow by 4 percent in 1997.

Interestingly, about half of U.S. trade with both Canada and Mexico takes place in just three industries: motor vehicles and parts, industrial machinery and computers; and electric/electronic equipment. Typically, the same industries are national leaders in both exports and imports. Regionalization under NAFTA appears to intensify local specialization within industries, rather than discretely allocating industries among countries. This will be another area for exploration in the larger NAFTA study.

Other Countries' Experiences

Given its success in promoting U.S. exports and helping Mexico recover, we believe the NAFTA standards of market openness should apply throughout the Hemisphere. Many of our trading partners have indicated their interest in accepting the obligations of a comprehensive free trade agreement like NAFTA, most importantly Chile.

The United States has the lowest tariffs and fewest non-tariff barriers in the region but many of our trading partners impose significant tariff barriers that can prohibit exports from entering their market. Recognizing the benefits of freer trade, many of the countries have banded together to form regional trading arrangements such as the Common Market of the South (Mercosur) and the Andean Community. As these trading blocs have come together, they have witnessed a significant increase in internal trade, just as we have in the NAFTA.

Since the United States is not part of these arrangements, our exporters are at a competitive disadvantage in those markets. Further, as these trading arrangements negotiate agreements between themselves, our exporters face additional competitive pressures and are losing market share. The Mercosur has completed an association agreement with Chile that provides free trade between Chile and Mercosur. Mexico and Chile have an agreement that will be made comprehensive this year, and Canada completed a Free Trade Agreement with Chile last year modeled on NAFTA. Mercosur will be negotiating with Colombia, Venezuela and Mexico this year, and has made overtures to the European Union and ASEAN.

Already, we are seeing the impact of these agreements as importers who can realize significant tariff savings source their supplies from countries that benefit from these free trade arrangements. For example, Southwest Bell recently chose to source from Northern Telecom in Canada $180 million in telecommunications equipment for a project in Chile rather than from U.S suppliers because it can save nearly $20 million in tariffs thanks to the Chile-Canada FTA. Washington state apple growers are losing market share in Chile to Mexico which also benefits from a free trade deal. Similar stories of shifts in sourcing from U.S. suppliers to countries that have free trade arrangements can be found throughout the hemisphere. Madame Chairman, the need to address these competitive disadvantages is one good reason why the United States is seeking to create a Free Trade Area of the Americas that is comprehensive and puts our firms and farms on an equal footing with their hemispheric competition.

Department of Commerce Export Services

The Department of Commerce is committed to providing quality service to U.S. businesses from all backgrounds and groups. In support of this effort, Commerce -- within its International Trade Administration unit -- has placed emphasis on providing export marketing support for small and medium-sized companies who are interested in pursuing business opportunities with our NAFTA partners. Our objective is to provide small and medium-sized firms with the information needed to take advantage of the major benefits made available under the NAFTA for doing business in Mexico and Canada. During 1994-97, ITA has focused its efforts on helping U.S. firms take advantage of the increased trade opportunities brought about by NAFTA. An integral part of accomplishing this goal is through the dissemination of trade related information. Let me give you a few examples of ITA's outreach efforts during the past two years.

o To respond to the thousands of business inquiries received each month we have established the **"NAFTA FACTS"** Information Hotline. The hotline is accessible 24 hours a day, seven days a week, and is free of charge. **"NAFTA FACTS"** is designed to provide accurate, up-to-date information to the business caller. **"NAFTA FACTS"** provided nearly 74,000 documents to the business community in 1996.

o ITA has brought on-line the **NAFTA Border Home Page** to provide a central location from which the business community can gather valuable information on the U.S. - Mexico border region via the information superhighway. Approximately 22,000 members of the business community have visited this web site.

o To increase the availability of information to U.S. exporters, especially small and medium-sized firms, ONA has developed the **NAFTA Home Page**. The NAFTA web site has not been in existence for a year yet, but based upon an average week's usage, total annual visits to this site will be about 47,000.

o To assist small and medium-sized firms in doing business in Mexico and Canada, ONA conducts telephone **business counseling** sessions. ONA conducted 12,000 business counseling sessions in 1996.

- o To help small and medium-sized U.S. firms take advantage of the benefits of NAFTA, the Department of Commerce in partnership with UPS and Federal Express sponsored a series of export workshops in over 100 cities. The **"Beyond Borders"** workshops reached a total audience of over 20,000 U.S. business executives.

- o We have focused our attention on alerting U.S. companies to the new opportunities under NAFTA. For example, U.S. firms have captured a steady share of the Canadian government procurement market, as a result of NAFTA's extension of the liberalized rules of the U.S.-Canada Free Trade Agreement. Many of the winners have been small and medium sized firms whose specific technology and expertise make them competitive. U.S. companies have expanded their sales in the face of cuts in Canadian government spending. U.S. companies in areas such as computer software, telecommunications and aviation and aerospace have done particularly well. In 1995 (last year for complete data), over 100 contracts falling under NAFTA's provisions on government procurement were given to U.S. firms.

CHART 1

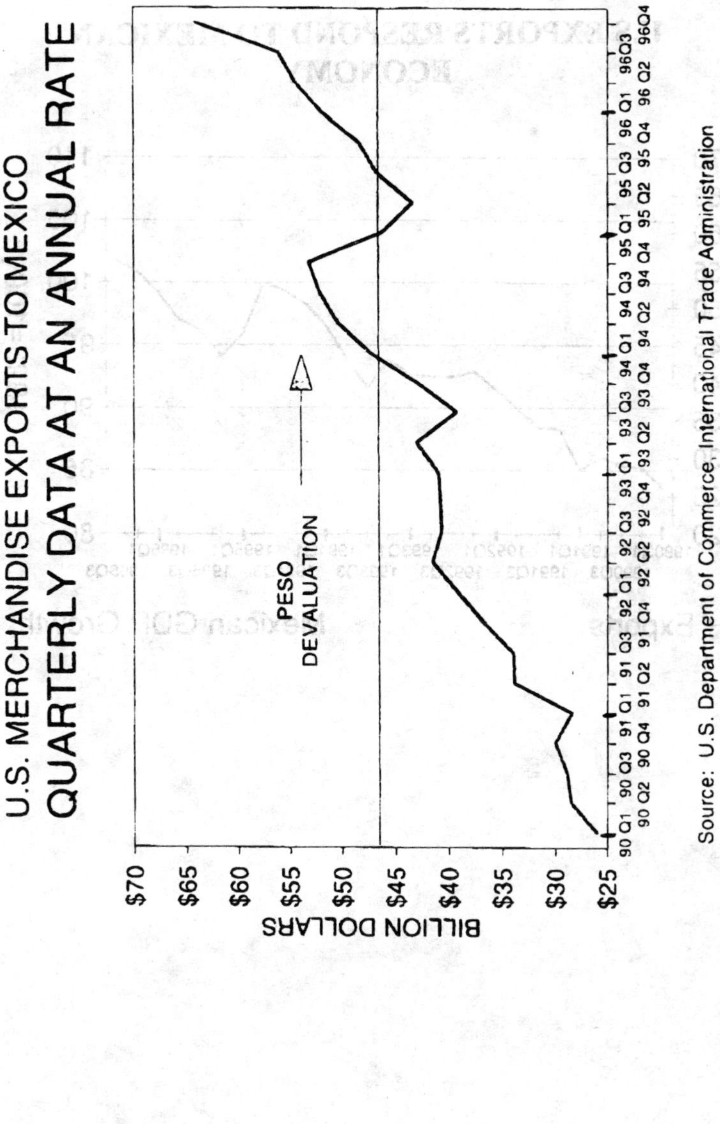

U.S. MERCHANDISE EXPORTS TO MEXICO
QUARTERLY DATA AT AN ANNUAL RATE
BILLION DOLLARS
$70
$65
$60
$55
$50
$45
$40
$35
$30
$25
PESO DEVALUATION
90 Q1 90 Q2 90 Q3 90 Q4 91 Q1 91 Q2 91 Q3 91 Q4 92 Q1 92 Q2 92 Q3 92 Q4 93 Q1 93 Q2 93 Q3 93 Q4 94 Q1 94 Q2 94 Q3 94 Q4 95 Q1 95 Q2 95 Q3 95 Q4 96 Q1 96 Q2 96Q3 96Q4
Source: U.S. Department of Commerce, International Trade Administration

CHART 2

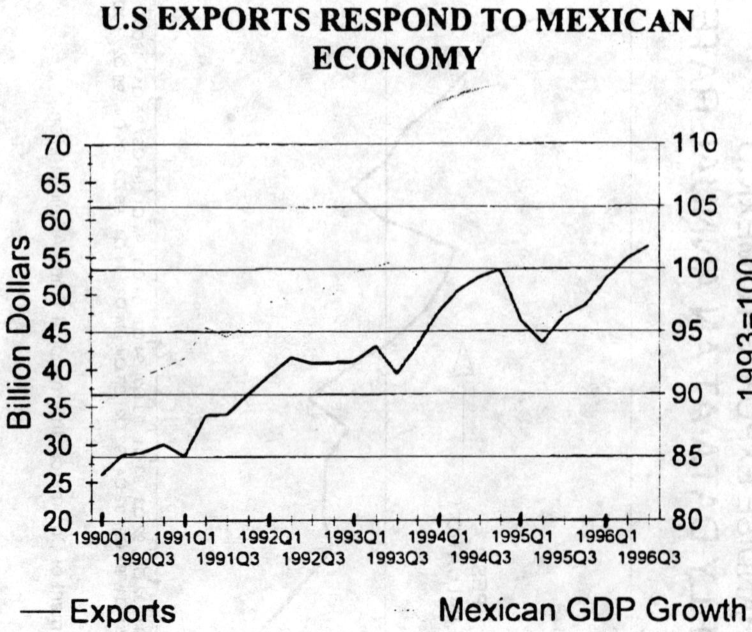
U.S EXPORTS RESPOND TO MEXICAN ECONOMY
70
65
60
55
50
45
40
35
30
25
20
Billion Dollars
110
105
100
95
90
85
80
1993=100
1990Q1
1991Q1
1992Q1
1993Q1
1994Q1
1995Q1
1996Q1
1990Q3
1991Q3
1992Q3
1993Q3
1994Q3
1995Q3
1996Q3
— Exports
Mexican GDP Growth

Testimony of Ron Carey
General President
International Brotherhood of Teamsters, AFL-CIO

House International Relations Subcommittee
on International Economic Policy and Trade

March 5, 1997

Mr. Chairman and members of the committee.

As general president of the 1.4 million member Teamsters Union, I want to thank the committee for hearing my testimony today. Too often the concerns of working families have been brushed aside in the rush to implement trade agreements. But it is precisely the concerns of workers that *should* be central to this debate. The purpose of trade agreements should be to raise the standards of living for all working families in the United States and other countries. They should protect workers and our environment, not simply pad the bottom lines of multinational corporations. When judged in this light, NAFTA does not measure up. It is an unfair trade deal that is destroying the future for working families here and in other countries.

The record of NAFTA's failed promises is becoming increasingly clear. In 1993, the year before NAFTA took effect, the U.S. had a trade *surplus* with Mexico. By 1996, that surplus had been wiped out by the largest Mexican trade *deficit* ever -- $16.3 billion. Added to the U.S. trade deficit with Canada, data from the U.S. Department of Commerce place the overall NAFTA deficit at more than $85 billion, making it the single biggest source of the United States' total trade deficit to all other countries.

As this trade deficit developed since 1994, more than 420,000 American jobs have been lost, according to a recent study by the Economic Policy Institute. These losses include more than 12,000 jobs in communications equipment manufacturing, more than 10,500 in computers, and nearly 50,000 in paper products as a result of NAFTA trade with Canada.

The Department of Labor's own statistics support the conclusion that jobs are being lost in record numbers. As of mid-February, the DOL says, 109,384 workers have qualified for job re-training or special extended unemployment benefits under NAFTA's Transitional Adjustment Assistance, a government program to help workers who lose their jobs because of the trade agreement. This represents only a small fraction of the NAFTA job loss because TAA is limited to certain types of workers and companies. Further, many workers displaced by NAFTA never file for TAA. The certification of workers and companies who qualify demonstrates just how sweeping NAFTA's impact has been -- as of January 18, 1996, the Labor Department had given TAA certification to workers from more than 700 companies in 48 states.

Meanwhile, NAFTA proponents continue to argue that jobs are being created, but these jobs are nowhere to be found. The consumer group Public Citizen recently examined the specific promises of U.S. job creation and/or increased American exports by 67 individual companies during the debate over NAFTA in 1993. Three years later, 60 of the 67 companies have not lived up to their promises. In fact, many of the companies have done just the opposite, shifting tens of thousands of American jobs to Mexico and increasing foreign imports.[1]

The final tragedy is that jobs not only are being lost, but the wages and benefits for those that remain are declining. NAFTA's supporters claimed in 1993 that passage would raise wages and create good jobs in both Mexico and the United States. But the opposite has been true. Real wages in the United States continue to fall despite the sustained economic recovery since the recession of the early 1990s. In 1994, NAFTA's first year, U.S. workers experienced the biggest drop in real hourly wages in history. And pay has continued to drop in each of the past two years. "As ugly as the NAFTA job loss data is, NAFTA's downward pressure on wages may be even more damaging," Public Citizen said in its February 1997 report.

Teamster members understand full well the pain of NAFTA. Just two weeks ago Osram Sylvania announced that it is laying off 145 Teamsters at its Danvers, Massachusetts plant and shifting the jobs to Mexico. This announcement came less than two years after the company's chief American officer wrote an opinion piece in the Boston Globe reiterating his opposition to NAFTA while extolling his workforce as "dedicated and motivated" and doing "a good job."[2] Unlike some companies that shift production to Mexico, Osram Sylvania is not modernizing its equipment; it is moving its decades-old production line from Massachusetts to Mexico. Its only motivation is bigger profits through exploiting Mexican workers. Osram will pay workers at its Mexican facility $8 a day, compared to $13 an hour for its current employees. Being "dedicated and motivated" and doing "a good job" is no longer enough to guarantee a decent job in America when government policy under NAFTA encourages the exploitation of low wages in other countries.

America's working families understand this betrayal as well, and their skepticism toward NAFTA is rising. A recent poll by the Bank of Boston showed that the American people believe free trade agreements cost jobs in the United States, and they are opposed to expanding new agreements to Latin America.[3] The poll also showed that the American people are growing increasingly hostile toward trade agreements. By nearly two-to-one, Americans believe foreign trade agreements do more to increase foreign imports than help U.S. exports. Three-quarters believe strong labor and environmental protections should be included in any new accords.

Under NAFTA, multinational corporations are the clear winners as they rush to exploit Mexican workers while destroying jobs in the United States. Working families in the U.S.

---

[1] NAFTA's Broken Promises: Failure to Create U.S. Jobs -- NAFTA's Three Year Reality: Spiraling Job Loss and Trade Deficits Instead of Job Creation, Public Citizen's Global Watch, February 1997.

[2] Boston Globe, North Weekly, April 16, 1995.

[3] Bank of Boston Poll, conducted November 1-4, 1996 by Wirthlin Worldwide.

and Mexico are the clear losers.

The Mexican economy and Mexican workers have been hit particularly hard since NAFTA's implementation. The value of the Mexican peso remains at just a third of its value prior to the trade agreement. The wages of Mexican workers in the maquiladoras, which were $5 a day on average prior to NAFTA, have plummeted to less than $3 because of the peso's devaluation. This has spurred even greater movement of jobs from the United States to Mexico as companies seek to take advantage of the devalued peso and the corresponding devaluation of wages. Employment in the maquiladoras has risen 48 percent since NAFTA was implemented.

It is not just poor Mexican workers along the border who have suffered. The Mexican middle class also has been hit hard. Since December 1994, nearly half of Mexican home mortgage-holders have defaulted on their loans, according to El Barzon, an organization of middle class debtors that is leading a consumer backlash in Mexico. The organization reports that more than 8 million Mexicans have fallen from the middle class into poverty in just the past two years. The economic devastation has shaken Mexico, sparking increased political instability and violence.

Other NAFTA promises have been broken as well. The General Accounting Office reported in Summer 1996 that pollution along the border had worsened despite assurances prior to NAFTA that the trade deal would improve environmental quality. And the agreement has not spurred a promised improvement in Mexican workplace democracy. Workers trying to organize independent unions have been fired by employers running vicious anti-union campaigns in violation of Mexican labor law and the NAFTA labor side agreement. Even in the United States, NAFTA is being used to bust unions and derail union organizing campaigns as companies use the threat of moving to Mexico to frighten workers, according to a study by Cornell University professor Kate Bronfenbrenner.[4]

Against this backdrop of failure and broken promises, political pressure is now being applied on President Clinton to lift a 14-month delay of NAFTA's trucking provisions, which were to have been implemented December 18, 1995. The trucking provisions would have given unsafe trucks from Mexico unlimited access immediately to the border states of Arizona, California, New Mexico and Texas, and to all of the United States and Canada in the year 2000. Currently, trucks from Mexico are confined to narrow strips along the border, where freight is picked up by American drivers for delivery in the United States.

Implementation of the trucking provisions would worsen NAFTA's economic harm to working families on both sides of the border. The big trucking firms already have set up partnerships with Mexican freight companies. They are poised to begin exploiting drivers

---

[4]Bronfenbrenner, Kate; Cornell University; The Effects of the Threat of Plan Closing on the Right of Workers to Organize, September 30, 1996.

from Mexico, who earn as little as $7 a day, and eliminating the jobs of American drivers.

In addition, the trucking part of NAFTA would undermine highway safety in the U.S. and increase drug trafficking from Mexico into the United States. Mexican trucks are three times as old as U.S. trucks and up to twice as heavy. They are not required to comply with the same emissions standards, and many are not properly insured to operate in the United States. Drivers from Mexico do not receive the same special training to transport hazardous materials as U.S. drivers -- despite the fact that up to 25 percent of trucks from Mexico carry hazardous materials -- and are not subject to the same tough rules for drug and alcohol testing. In Texas alone, there are 1. 9 million border crossings from Mexico a year, according to the General Accounting Office. Fewer than one of every 200 trucks from Mexico is inspected at the border. Of those that are checked, half are put out of service because they are unsafe, according to the GAO.[5] Problems include improperly licensed and underage drivers, broken suspensions, substandard tires, inoperable brakes, and unsecured loads, including toxic and hazardous materials.

Enforcement of trucking safety provisions are not in place at the border. In Laredo, Texas, for example, the busiest entry point in the United States with as many as 4,500 trucks crossing from Mexico every day, there are just three truck inspection lanes and one scale. In early October a member of my staff visited Laredo and observed the border operation. With the exception of one 15- to 20-minute period, he did not see a single truck inspected. In fact, the inspection lanes were blocked by Texas Department of Public Safety vehicles, and truck traffic from Mexico was diverted around the inspection area.

Just as troubling was the U.S. Customs area at Laredo, where the average inspection time is three to four minutes. During this period, the customs agents are supposed to check a driver's border crossing card, insurance, ICC permit, freight paperwork and compliance with literally hundreds of Customs and other regulations. Only rarely do the agents look inside the trucks, despite the fact that Mexico is one of the biggest suppliers of illicit drugs to the United States. Implementing the trucking provisions will make it even easier for traffickers to move drugs across the border and into our neighborhoods and schools.

Given NAFTA's failure for working people, it make no sense to implement the NAFTA trucking provisions and allow these problems to take hold in another industry. And it makes no sense to pursue an accord that will undermine highway safety and increase the flow of drugs into the United States. The trucking delay should be made permanent, and the trucking provisions should be re-negotiated to protect working families on both sides of the border.

Further, I urge Congress to refuse the administration's request for fast track authority to

---

[5] Commercial Trucking -- Safety and Infrastructure Issues Under the North American Free Trade Agreement, General Accounting Office, February 1996.

extend NAFTA to Chile and other Latin American countries. The huge problems created by NAFTA should be solved before we even consider expanding the trade deal to other countries.

Working families have already been hurt enough by NAFTA. Don't make them pay an even higher price for a flawed and broken agreement.

Statement of the U.S. Chamber of Commerce

ON: REPORT CARD ON NAFTA

TO: THE SUBCOMMITTEE ON INTERNATIONAL ECONOMIC POLICY AND TRADE of the HOUSE COMMITTEE ON INTERNATIONAL RELATIONS

DATE: MARCH 5, 1997

BY: WILLARD A. WORKMAN

The Chamber's mission is to advance human progress through an economic, political and social system based on individual freedom, incentive, initiative, opportunity and responsibility.

The U.S. Chamber of Commerce is the world's largest business federation representing an underlying membership of more than three million businesses and organizations of every size, sector, and region.

More than 96 percent of the Chamber's members are small businesses with 100 or fewer employees, 71 percent of which have 10 or fewer employees. Yet, virtually all of the nation's largest companies are also active members. We are particularly cognizant of the problems of smaller businesses, as well as issues facing the business community at large.

Besides representing a cross-section of the American business community in terms of number of employees, the Chamber represents a wide management spectrum by type of business and location. Each major classification of American business -- manufacturing, retailing, services, construction, wholesaling, and finance -- numbers more than 10,000 members. Also, the Chamber has substantial membership in all 50 states.

The Chamber's international reach is substantial as well. It believes that global interdependence provides an opportunity, not a threat. In addition to the U.S. Chamber of Commerce's 78 American Chambers of Commerce abroad, an increasing number of members are engaged in the export and import of both goods and services and have ongoing investment activities. The Chamber favors strengthened international competitiveness and opposes artificial U.S. and foreign barriers to international business.

Positions on national issues are developed by a cross-section of Chamber members serving on committees, subcommittees, and task forces. Currently, some 1,800 business people participate in this process.

STATEMENT
on the
NORTH AMERICAN FREE TRADE AGREEMENT
before the
SUBCOMMITTEE ON INTERNATIONAL ECONOMIC POLICY AND TRADE
of the
HOUSE COMMITTEE ON INTERNATIONAL RELATIONS

by
Willard A. Workman
March 5, 1997

Thank you, Madam Chairwoman. On behalf of the US Chamber of Commerce, thank you for this opportunity to testify before this Subcommittee on International Economic Policy and Trade. I am Willard Workman, Vice President, International, of the US Chamber of Commerce. As you know, the US Chamber is the world's largest business federation, representing an underlying membership of more than three million businesses and organizations of every size, sector, and region.

I am pleased to report that the North American Free Trade Agreement (NAFTA) itself gets an A.

This grade is based on the fact that the members of the US Chamber of Commerce are confident that NAFTA has:

1) Increased trade, which creates jobs;
2) Built a solid foundation for economic growth in the United States; and
3) Begun a program for sustained economic strength in the Americas.

At the same time, I would give the governments of the United States and Mexico a B+ for the way they have implemented certain parts the agreement to date.

Increasing Exports and Creating Jobs

Over the last few years, exports and small business have driven US job growth. Trade liberalizing pacts like NAFTA are the very best means of joining these two job engines. By harnessing the innovation of entrepreneurs and lowering trade barriers in markets growing much faster than ours here at home, free trade policy is an essential part of creating jobs in the high-growth markets of the developing world. Trade is not, after all, a zero sum game. As trade grows, around the world, all who participate benefit.

Mexico and Canada represent two of the markets American companies and their workers now have which are open to the goods they produce. NAFTA was an important step in opening opportunities for American companies looking to grow their businesses.

During Congressional debate of the merits of the NAFTA, its many supporters said that it would increase exports and create jobs. Today, when looking at the trade statistics, you can see that this has, in fact, been the case.

Total US exports to both Canada and Mexico last year topped $190 billion, a 9% increase over 1995 exports of $173.5 billion. To give you a before and after snapshot of the US - Mexico trade relationship, in 1993, US exports to Mexico stood at $42 billion. Last year, our exports to Mexico exceeded $57 billion, a 36% increase.

These export figures have risen to such tremendous levels because NAFTA created new, more favorable rules for American companies looking to export to Mexico and Canada. An example of the benefits derived can be found in the automotive industry. Prior to NAFTA, American automobile manufacturers wishing to sell autos in Mexico faced countless restrictions. Prohibitive tariffs and rules which required manufacturing operations in Mexico before exporting from the United States to that country were quite onerous and restrictive. In 1994, the first year of NAFTA, the automobile industry exported just 57,500 units. Last year, an impressive 86,000 units traveled across the border into Mexico, and increase of nearly 50%.

Stable Rules for Growth

With the implementation of NAFTA on January 1, 1994, a new set of trade and investment rules went into place across North America. Businesses of all sizes have a clear and consistent set of rules that they must play by in the NAFTA market. It is these predictable rules for doing business in Mexico and Canada that have helped give US companies a leg up over their Asian and European competitors trying to export into the growing Mexican market.

A good example of the benefits of clear trade rules resulted from the Mexican peso devaluation. As we all know, unsound fiscal policy caused the government of Mexico to devalue its currency in late 1994. As a result, the Mexican economy shrank 7% during Mexico's worst economic crisis since 1932, and US exports fell nearly 9%.

In an effort to raise revenue, the Mexican government looked at its international trade policy and found that it could raise tariffs on European and Asian exporters. The resulting tariff hike caused their exports to fall between 20 and 30 %. However, due to its NAFTA obligations, Mexico could not unilaterally increase tariffs on US goods. As a result, US exports did not fall nearly as dramatically; instead, NAFTA worked to protect over 700,000 US jobs. NAFTA's predictable rules worked like an insurance policy for our small and medium sized exporters during the peso crisis.

Furthermore, despite the economic crisis, US companies kept a strong foothold in the Mexican market. In fact, US companies have increased their market share, from 70% in 1994 to 75% in 1995.

All of this underscores the important stabilizing effect that NAFTA had on the bilateral trade relationship between the US and Mexico during its time of crisis. The pact clearly provided a strong policy framework for Mexico when its fiscal house fell into disrepair.

NAFTA also helped accellerate Mexico's recovery for the crisis. Because Mexico maintained its committment to open markets, the country's economy has started to grow again. In fact, Mexico's economy grew 4.5% last year. As a result, US exports increased 23% last year, a $10 billion increase in sales, while our 1996 imports from Mexico grew 18%. This shows that NAFTA's rules create a win-win scenario for US and Mexican business, both in good times and bad times.

NAFTA Sets a Course for the Future of the Americas

We cannot, however, complacently sit back and merely smile at the positive results NAFTA has wrought to date. Instead, we must press for full implementation of the trilateral agreement, and build on it to create a Hemisphere-wide free trade area.

Implementation of any agreement as comprehensive as NAFTA is an ambitious and difficult task. At the same time, many important items remain outstanding. First and foremost is the ongoing bilateral dispute over cross-border trucking. An inefficient border raises the cost of transporting goods, a cost which is inevitably passed along to consumers. It seems that the United States has finally developed the political will to seek implementation of this part of the agreement, which was suspended on December 18, 1995. Therefore, the US Chamber urges both the Mexican and US governments to continue making progress toward resolution of this issue. The current system is cumbersome, cost-prohibitive, and frustrating for truckers and the many businesses using land transportation to get their goods to the Mexican market.

This dispute has also held up progress on a number of other fronts. Among the issues held hostage by the trucking dispute are access to the Mexican market for small package delivery companies, and the issuance of new rules authorizing the use of standard 53-foot trailers in Mexico. We must resolve these issues quickly so that companies across North America can benefit from the trilateral agreement.

One other piece of "unfinished business" is tariff acceleration. NAFTA includes a provision which allows the governments to agree to lower tariffs on specific goods before they are scheduled to be lowered under the accord. We urge the governments of North America to begin tariff acceleration negotiations again, and take the opportunity to lower the tariffs paid on goods traveling across North America.

It is essential that this movement toward zero tariff barriers be implemented not only in North America, but across the Americas. The US Chamber of Commerce has been an ardent supporter of the Free Trade Area of the Americas concept proposed by President Clinton and agreed to by the 34 democratically elected Heads of State of the Western Hemisphere.

In the Americas, we have nearly unanimous agreement that free trade builds jobs and promotes economic growth. The United States must lead this effort in order to ensure that when the rules of the Free Trade Area of the Americas are written—and you can rest assured that they will be—the interests of American companies of all sizes are represented by our government's policy-makers. Unfortunately, without fast-track trade negotiating authority, the United States is forced to sit on the sidelines, while other nations proceed to negotiate their own trade pacts. For example, Chile's trade deals with Mercosur, Mexico and Canada have lowered the tariffs that our competitors in Canada, Brazil, Argentina and Mexico pay when selling their goods to Chile. We know that our competitors in Europe are urging the European Union to negotiate its own special trading relationship with these countries.

Therefore, Madam Chair, now that we're grading NAFTA, let's also set up our lesson plan for tomorrow. Make Chile the fourth member of the accord, and set a course for economic growth and prosperity in the United States.

With that I will conclude my formal remarks. I would be happy to respond to any questions you or other members of the committee might have.

Statement of

Paul J. DiMare

The DiMare Companies
Homestead, Florida

(305) 245-4211

Before The

U.S. House of Representatives

Committee on International Relations

Subcommittee on International Economic Policy and Trade

"Report Card on NAFTA"
Room 2172
Rayburn House Office Building
Washington, D.C.

2:00 pm
Wednesday, March 5, 1997

By: Paul J. DiMare

My name is Paul DiMare, I am President of the DiMare Companies in Homestead, Florida. I would like to thank you for the opportunity to appear before this subcommittee today and talk about the problem of the Florida winter vegetable industry, particularly since the NAFTA treaty has been implemented. In addition to my statement, I would also request that you include the attached appendixes for the record.

Today, our industry, which is now composed of less than 300 producers is truly an endangered species. Before I begin talking about NAFTA and our industry trade problems, I would like to tell you a little bit about my own family business. The DiMare companies have been in the produce business for over 70 years. We have branches in Homestead, Tampa and Ruskin, Florida. We also have operations in South Carolina, California and Boston, MA.

I have five sons, four of them are actively involved in our family business. At one time, we farmed over 14,000 acres of tomatoes and winter vegetables. The Florida farming operation not only created opportunity for my family, but it also created thousands of jobs for farmworkers. I would like to believe that the DiMare Homestead operation made a big impact on the South Dade community. In fact, in 1992 when hurricane Andrew devastated the area, we did not hesitate for one moment and quickly rebuilt our packinghouse and other infrastructure in Dade County. Today, because of unfair trade practices by Mexican winter vegetable producers, our operations have dwindled to less than 5000 acres.

When NAFTA was proposed, it was sold to the U.S. Congress and the American people on the basis that it would enhance our trade surplus by billions of dollars and thus create thousands of new jobs. That has not happened. In fact today, few politicians like to talk about NAFTA, perhaps because the 1992 U.S. trade surplus with Mexico of $5 billion turned into a $15 billion deficit in 1995 and about the same amount in 1996.

NAFTA was a way for American bankers and business people to recover the billions they had earlier lent to the Mexican government and to some Mexican companies. Today, Mexico has 24 billionaires excluding drug lords and corrupt officials. Much of this money was siphoned from loans made by American banks.

In 1993, when General Motors proposed to close its plant near Dallas and move it back to Michigan, Governor Ann Richards of Texas pleaded with GM hierarchy and succeeded in retaining the factory. She shuddered at the thought of GM moving out of Texas and back to Michigan, but it suited her fine if GM moved some plants out of Michigan into Mexico.

Governor Pete Wilson had been doing his best to retain industry in California. Yet he was happy to let U.S. industry elsewhere move south of the border. As Governor of Arkansas in the 1980's Bill Clinton offered tax concessions to attract business into his state. But as President, he rejoiced at the thought of American Companies moving to Mexico.

We have lost about 300,000 jobs the first year with NAFTA and real wages have fallen with them. Inflation adjusted salaries in the U.S. have been generally on the decline since 1972. But they had bottomed by 1992 and were starting to turn up. Now look at what has happened to the U.S. and Mexican real wages after the adoption of NAFTA in January 1994. The U.S. real average earnings had bottomed in December 1992 at $253 and rose to $ 257 by the day NAFTA went into effect. Immediately, they started to fall even as the rate of unemployment inched down. Just before the adoption of NAFTA on the first day of 1994, real wages had been constantly rising in both countries. Soon after U.S. real earnings inched down and those in Mexico crashed. In the absence of the trade deficit, labor demand would be larger and U.S. real wages would be much greater.

What is happening to our winter vegetables industry is very much what is happening to other industries across the country. The winter vegetable industry is worth saving, because it is one of the few segments of American agriculture that has never received government subsidies. And it provides thousands of unskilled jobs.

Our problem is mostly due to sales below cost of production and although dumping product on the U.S. market has been a practice of Mexican producers for over 20 years, the situation has gotten much worse since the implementation of NAFTA. The tariffs rollbacks on tomatoes have not been a major factor, because they did not amount to much to begin with (see Appx. H). However, the increased production by Mexican growers, which can not be absorbed by U.S. consumption without disrupting the market, and the drastic peso devaluation in December of 1994, have had a devastating effect on the Florida tomato and winter vegetable industry (see Appx. A,B,C,D,E,F,G).

Over 200 Florida winter vegetables farmers have gone out of business since 1993. During the same period over 6,000 farmworker jobs have been lost in Florida. Mexican growers pay an average of $ 4.00 per day. However many growers bring in Indian workers from Southern Mexico who work for as little as $ 3.00 per day. Florida farmworkers receive an average of $ 6.77 an hour (USDA/ERS 3/96) or $ 60.00 per day.

Florida growers must comply with strict U.S. government regulations while Mexican growers use child labor and unregistered/U.S. banned pesticides.

Even if laws are applicable, they are not enforced. Unsanitary conditions in the production and packaging of fruits and vegetables are also commonly practiced in Mexico. The double standard of pesticide use in Mexico is indefensible. If a pesticide is illegal in the U.S., why is a foreign import containing the illegal substance considered safe ? This double standard affect, most foods imported into our country. The American consumer is being deceived by not knowing the facts. Perhaps, if U.S. laws were enforced we could resolve the illegal pesticide issue.

As most of you have probably read recently, corruption is widespread in Mexico. The government of Mexico is one of the most corrupt governments in this hemisphere. And by New York based Freedom House's own definition, Mexico is not a total democracy. Drug traffic is also playing a major factor in our industry.

While most of the Mexican producers are legitimate farmers, there are several huge operations that have surfaced in the past 5 years that no one seems to know who they are or where they came from. For some time now, U.S. growers have suspected that the surge in Mexican tomato and winter vegetables was being financed by drug money, given the Mexican's ability to dump product in the U.S. market. This concern has been reported by major news outlets, including the Washington Post and the New York Times. Carlos Cabal Peniche, a Mexican fugitive, who at one time owned Del Monte Fresh, a Coral Gables, Florida based company made over $300 million in loans to several Sinaloa tomato growers. These loans have never been paid back to Mexican banks and probably will never be repaid. NAFTA was supposed to eliminate all subsidies so we could all complete on the same level field. The U.S. Government, and particularly Congress, ought to investigate these operators to find out if illegal drug smugglers are simply laundering money. These operations could well be exporting 25% of the total Mexican fruit and vegetable exports. This is a huge hidden subsidy that makes it impossible to compete against.

To date, the promises of the NAFTA agreement have not been fulfilled. The safeguards designed to protect vegetable growers in Florida have not worked. Last year, it became necessary for the Florida industry to file an antidumping action against Mexican tomato exporters. In October of 1996, the U.S. Department of Commerce released their preliminary findings. Preliminary figures showed dumping margins averaging 17%. This would have resulted in Mexican importers having to post bonds of between 70 to 140 million U.S. dollars. As a result, the Department of Commerce and the Mexican producers entered into a landmark suspension agreement.

Under the agreement Mexican growers agreed not to sell tomatoes in the U.S. market below 20.6 cents per pound. In return, Commerce suspended the investigation.

The agreement was working well until recently. But because of quality problems the Mexicans began adjusting the price on most loads of tomatoes, thus circumventing the agreement. To date, despite a clear violation of the agreement, the U.S. Department of Commerce has refused to issue a clarification on the matter. In the meantime, Mexican producers continue to dump product on the U.S. market.

The industry is currently working with the U.S. Customs Service to put systems into place that will improve enforcement. However, we are finding out that staffing requirements are insufficient and Customs and USDA do not have the staff to conduct inspections properly.

The American consumer has a vital interest in the importation of goods into this country, particularly fruits and vegetables. The 1990 Farm Bill described our interest as follows: "Fruits and vegetables, and specialty crops are a vital and important source of nutrition for the general health and nutrition of the people of the United States". American consumers are concerned about price, quality and food safety. And ever since the 1974 OPEC oil embargo, the consumer has been concerned about the self-sufficiency of our country. Once the few Florida farmers now left are out of business, we will be totally dependent on Mexican imports. I do not believe this was what Congress intended when they passed NAFTA.

Florida farmers deserve a fair deal from the U.S. government and an opportunity to compete in the marketplace. This opportunity to compete does not require a loosening of standards or an increase in retail price (see Appx. I). What is required is the application of laws against unfair trade practices by Mexico, primarily, the antidumping act.

Our industry is particularly sensitive about future trade pacts in this hemisphere mainly because this could further stress the inspection services and have an impact on the quality of the U.S. food supply. Before the U.S. government proceeds with other major trade agreements such as the inclusion of Chile into NAFTA and the Free Trade Agreement of the Americas (FTAA), the U.S. congress ought to examine what has happened to our industry and other U.S. industries. If these industries are not safeguarded, We will be solely dependent on imports. This is not in the best interest of the citizens of the United States.

This hearing is entitled: "Report Card on NAFTA". In reviewing what has happened to the Florida winter vegetable industry, I would have to give NAFTA a failing grade. The NAFTA agreement and its side effects, have been tough and most importantly, unfair on Florida farmers, suppliers and farmworkers.

Again, I thank you for the opportunity to appear before you.

Appendix A.

Tomatoes

(25-Pound Carton)

Competitive Growing Season Shipments, Annual Change and U.S. Market Share

	1991-92 Season		1992-93 Season			1993-94 Season			1994-95 Season			1995-96 Season		
Region	Shipments	Percent Market	Shipments	Percent Change	Percent Market	Shipments	Percent Change	Percent Market	Shipments	Percent Change	Percent Market	Shipments	Percent Change	Percent Market
Florida	67,829,000	69.4	56,887,000	- 16.1	56.4	52,810,000	- 7.2	51.6	47,471,000	- 10.1	45.2	37,265,000	- 21.5	35.1
Mexico	12,640,000	12.9	28,333,000	+ 124.2	28.0	31,239,000	+10.6	30.5	42,742,000	+ 36.8	40.7	52,539,000	+ 22.9	49.5
California	17,278,000	17.7	15,789,000	- 8.6	15.6	18,331,000	+ 16.1	17.9	14,791,000	- 19.3	14.1	16,265,000	+ 10.0	15.4
Total	97,747,000	100.0	101,009,000	+ 3.3	100.0	102,380,000	+ 1.4	100.0	105,004,000	+ 2.6	100.0	106,069,000	+ 1.0	100.0

Compiled by the Florida Department of Agriculture
(From Marketing Florida Vegetable Summary – Federal/State Market News, Orlando)

(c:\wpdocs\tables/tomatoes.trn)

11/05/96

Appendix B.

Bell Peppers

(28-Pound Carton)

Competitive Growing Season Shipments, Annual Change and U.S. Market Share

Region	1991-92 Season		1992-93 Season			1993-94 Season			1994-95 Season			1995-96 Season		
	Shipments	Percent Market	Shipments	Percent Change	Percent Market	Shipments	Percent Change	Percent Market	Shipments	Percent Change	Percent Market	Shipments	Percent Change	Percent Market
Florida	11,798,000	55.8	9,201,000	- 22.0	47.6	9,790,000	+ 6.4	48.9	8,449,000	- 13.7	45.7	8,283,000	- 2.0	39.6
Mexico	2,459,000	11.6	8,141,000	+ 231.1	42.1	8,773,000	+ 7.7	43.8	8,939,000	+ 1.9	48.3	11,647,000	+ 30.1	55.7
Texas	2,017,000	9.5	1,667,000	- 17.6	8.6	1,224,000	- 26.5	6.1	1,118,000	- 8.7	6.0	973,000	- 12.9	4.7
California	4,853,000	23.1	326,000	- 93.3	1.7	232,000	- 28.8	1.2	None			None		
Total	21,127,000	100.0	19,325,000	- 8.5	100.0	20,019,000	+ 3.5	100.0	18,506,000	- 7.6	100.0	20,903,000	+ 13.0	100.0

Compiled by the Florida Department of Agriculture
(From Marketing Florida Vegetable Summary--Federal/State Market News, Orlando)

(c:\wpdoc\tables\peppers.trn)

11/05/96

Appendix C.

Cucumbers

(55-Pound Bushel)

Competitive Growing Season Shipments, Annual Change and U.S. Market Share

Region	1991-92 Season		1992-93 Season			1993-94 Season			1994-95 Season			1995-96 Season		
	Shipments	Percent Market	Shipments	Percent Change	Percent Market	Shipments	Percent Change	Percent Market	Shipments	Percent Change	Percent Market	Shipments	Percent Change	Percent Market
Florida	6,009,000	44.9	5,368,000	- 10.7	37.7	4,095,000	- 23.7	30.7	4,121,000	+ 0.6	31.7	3,508,000	- 14.9	20.9
Mexico	6,904,000	44.1	7,546,000	+ 27.8	52.9	8,124,000	+ 7.7	60.9	7,784,000	- 4.2	59.8	12,027,000	+ 54.5	71.6
Georgia	1,049,000	7.8	951,000	- 9.3	6.7	940,000	- 1.2	7.0	782,000	- 16.8	6.0	1,131,000	+44.6	6.7
Texas	343,000	3.2	379,000	- 12.7	2.7	181,000	- 52.2	1.4	331,000	+ 82.9	2.5	136,000	- 58.9	0.8
Total	13,396,000	100.0	14,244,000	+ 6.3	100.0	13,340,000	- 6.3	100.0	13,018,000	- 2.4	100.0	16,802,000	+ 29.1	100.0

Compiled by the Florida Department of Agriculture
(From Marketing Florida Vegetable Summary -- Federal/State Market News, Orlando)

(c:\wpdocs\tables\cukes.trn)

11/5/96

Appendix D

Eggplant

(33-Pound Bushel)

Competitive Growing Season Shipments, Annual Change and U.S. Market Share

	1991-92 Season		1992-93 Season			1993-94 Season			1994-95 Season			1995-96 Season		
Region	Shipments	Percent Market	Shipments	Percent Change	Percent Market	Shipments	Percent Change	Percent Market	Shipments	Percent Change	Percent Market	Shipments	Percent Change	Percent Market
Florida	1,404,000	53.5	1,261,000	- 10.2	47.4	1,098,000	- 12.9	45.5	1,010,000	- 8.0	39.6	764,000	- 24.4	25.9
Mexico	1,221,000	46.5	1,400,000	+ 14.7	52.6	1,313,000	- 6.2	54.5	1,541,000	+ 17.4	60.4	2,188,000	+ 41.9	74.1
Total	2,625,000	100.0	2,661,000	+ 1.4	100.0	2,411,000	- 9.8	100.0	2,551,000	+ 5.8	100.0	2,952,000	+ 15.7	100.0

Compiled by the Florida Department of Agriculture
(From Marketing Florida Vegetable Summary -- Federal/State Market News, Orlando)

(c:\wpdocs\tables\eggplant.trn)

11/05/96

Squash
(33-Pound Bushel)

Competitive Growing Season Shipments, Annual Change and U.S. Market Share

Region	1991-92 Season		1992-93 Season			1993-94 Season			1994-95 Season			1995-96 Season		
	Shipments	Percent Market	Shipments	Percent Change	Percent Market	Shipments	Percent Change	Percent Market	Shipments	Percent Change	Percent Market	Shipments	Percent Change	Percent Market
Florida	4,459,000	62.6	3,025,000	- 32.2	32.0	2,425,000	-3.3	27.8	2,559,000	- 12.7	26.0	1,964,000	- 23.3	18.0
Califonia	5,000	0.1	53,000	+ 960.0	0.6	19,000	- 64.1	0.2	22,000	+ 15.8	0.2	13,000	- 40.9	0.1
Mexico & Texas	2,657,000	37.3	6,371,000	+ 139.4	67.4	7,589,000	+ 19.1	72.0	7,259,000	- 4.3	73.8	8,963,000	+ 23.5	81.9
Total	7,121,000	100.0	9,449,000	+ 32.1	100.0	10,537,000	+ 11.5	100.0	9,840,000	- 6.6	100.0	10,940,000	+ 11.2	100.0

Compiled by the Florida Department of Agriculture
(From Marketing Florida Vegetable Summary -- Federal/State Market News, Orlando)

(c:\wpdocs\tables/squash.trn)

11/05/96

Appendix F.

Sweet Corn
(42-Pound Crate)

Competitive Growing Season Shipmnts, Annual Change and U.S. Market Share

Region	1991-92 Season		1992-93 Season			1993-94 Season			1994-95 Season			1995-96 Season		
	Shipments	Percent Market	Shipments	Percent Change	Percent Market	Shipments	Percent Change	Percent Market	Shipments	Percent Change	Percent Market	Shipments	Percent Change	Percent Market
Florida	9,474,000	92.3	6,552,000	- 30.8	78.5	7,160,000	- 9.3	84.1	7,053,000	- 1.5	70.5	6,536,000	- 7.3	64.7
Mexico	649,000	6.3	651,000	+ 0.3	8.0	675,000	+ 3.7	7.9	984,000	+ 45.7	9.8	1,319,000	+ 34.0	13.1
California & Arizona	139,000	1.4	1,130,000	+ 712.9	13.5	679,000	- 39.9	8.0	1,972,000	+ 190.4	19.7	2,242,000	+ 13.7	22.2
Total	10,262,000	100.0	8,333,000	- 18.8	100.0	8,514,000	+ 2.2	100.0	10,009,000	+ 17.2	100.0	10,097,000	+ 0.9	100.0

Compiled by the Florida Department of Agriculture
(From Marketing Florida Vegetable Summary -- Federal/State Market News, Orlando)

(c:\wpdocs\tables\corn.tm)

11/05/96

Appendix G.

Beans

(30-Pound Bushel)

Competitive Growing Season Shipments, Annual Change and U.S. Market Share

	1991-92 Season		1992-93 Season			1993-94 Season			1994-95 Season			1995-96 Season		
Region	Shipments	Percent Market	Shipments	Percent Change	Percent Market	Shipments	Percent Change	Percent Market	Shipments	Percent Change	Percent Market	Shipments	Percent Change	Percent Market
Florida	3,709,000	82.2	2,671,000	- 28.0	72.9	2,816,000	+ 5.4	77.7	2,838,000	+ 0.8	72.9	2,117,000	- 25.4	59.2
Mexico	801,000	17.8	992,000	+ 23.8	27.1	806,000	- 18.7	22.3	1,057,000	+ 31.3	27.1	1,447,000	+ 36.4	40.6
Total	4,510,00	100.0	3,663,000	- 18.8	100.0	3,622,000	- 1.1	100.0	3,895,000	+ 7.5	100.0	3,564,000	- 8.5	100.0

Compiled by the Florida Department of Agriculture
(From Marketing Florida Vegetable Summary--Federal/State Market News, Orlando)

(c:\wpdocs\tables\beans.tm)

11/05/96

Appendix H.

Mexican Tomato Tarriff Rate Quota (TRQ)
(November 15-February 29)

Date	1994-95 Shipments (Kilograms)	1994-95 Percent of TRQ	1995-96 Shipments (Kilograms)	1995-96 Percent of TRQ	1996-97 Shipments (Kilograms)	1996-97 Percent of TRQ
Nov. 15-30	6,329,545	3.7	19,420,455	10.9	18,030,481	9.9
December	29,159,000	16.9	52,295,454	29.5	54,692,461	29.9
January	64,443,181	37.4	83,306,818	46.9	99,394,448	54.3
February	103,806,818	60.2	122,352,272	68.9	*58,117,119	31.8
Totals	203,718,634	118.2	277,374,999	156.3	230,234,509	125.9
TRQ	172,300,000	100.0	177,469,000	100.0	182,793,000	100.0

* Through February 12, 1997
Compiled by the Florida Department of Agriculture
(From Federal/State Market News Service)

c:\wpdoc\tables\TRQ.97

11/26/96

Appendix I.

FLORIDA AVERAGE FARM PRICE AND AVERAGE FLORIDA RETAIL PRICES

Week of December 9, 1996

(Average Price Per Pound)

Commodity	Farm Price	Retail Price	Price Markup	Percent Markup
Snap Beans	$0.35	$1.04	$0.69	197.1
Cucumbers	$0.11	$0.63	$0.52	472.7
Sweet Corn*	$0.15	$0.42	$0.27	180.0
Eggplant	$0.19	$1.06	$0.87	458.1
Yellow Squash	$0.21	$1.01	$0.80	380.9
Bell Peppers	$0.24	$0.86	$0.62	258.3
Tomatoes	$0.24	$1.25	$1.01	420.8
Zucchini	$0.16	$0.99	$0.83	518.7

* Price Per Ear

Compiled by the Florida Department of Agriculture and Consumer Services

PAUL J. DiMARE
DiMare Companies
Homestead, FL

Paul J. DiMare was born in Boston, MA in 1941. The DiMare Companies have been in the produce business for 75 years. Paul J. DiMare moved to South Florida in 1964 to take over the reigns of the DiMare Company's operations. The DiMare Companies operate in Homestead, FL; Ruskin, FL; Tampa, FL; Johns Island, S.C; Boston, MA, and Newman and Indio, CA.

Mr. DiMare has been an industry activist since his early days in Florida. In 1978 he was one of the industry leaders that brought an antidumping action against Mexico for the sale of winter vegetables at below cost of production in the U.S. market. This was the first time ever, that an antidumping action had been filed for a perishable commodity. Mr. DiMare is a past President of the Florida Tomato Exchange and the Florida Tomato Committee. Mr. DiMare is presently Chairman of the Florida Farmers & Suppliers Coalition, Inc.

Mr. DiMare is married and has five sons. He resides in Coral Gables, Florida.

Written Submission for the Record

Hearings
"Report Card on NAFTA"
International Economic Policy and Trade Subcommittee
International Relations Committee
US House of Representatives

FRESH PRODUCE ASSOCIATION OF THE AMERICAS

Nogales, Arizona

James Cathey, Chairman
Lee Frankel, President

March 5, 1997

Members of the Fresh Produce Association of the Americas (FPAA) have seen and experienced the many benefits, as well as the problems, of NAFTA. Having said that, however, as a trade association for American businesses (involved in the shipping, distribution, and sales of Mexican produce and related products), FPAA believes the overall report card on NAFTA should be an "A." Perhaps some teachers might comment on "behavior," but all would emphasize "Shows promise."

We must drop our obsession with expecting dramatic, immediate changes resulting from NAFTA. Just as a teacher does not give up hope when a student fails to quickly master a course, we must see NAFTA as a process, not as an end result. The meaningful report card on NAFTA is the college degree, not the reports at the end of each term.

NAFTA seems to have become an easy place to focus blame for our economic problems, whatever the real reasons for them might be. For example, if there is an increase of fresh tomatoes (or other agricultural products) from Mexico, NAFTA is cited as the cause. *We believe more attention should be focused on possible other reasons and causes.*

Specifically in the case of fresh winter tomatoes, statistics show that imports from Mexico have increased. NAFTA is not the reason for the increase, however. *NAFTA did not create enough changes to significantly affect tomato imports in a matter of few years. Even with NAFTA, tomato imports are still subject to tariffs, two seasonal tariff rate quotas, and all the regulations that result from the tomato marketing order in Florida.*

As presented in testimony before the Subcommittee by Mr. Paul DiMare, *Florida tomato growers filed a number of trade-related actions against Mexican tomato imports.* Two "escape clause" petitions were filed, but the US International Trade Commission

(USITC) found that imports were not injuring Florida tomato growers or the Florida tomato industry. A second petition was withdrawn before a final ruling was handed down. Florida tomato growers then filed an antidumping complaint. In the politics-above-all world of 1996, the Commerce Department handed down a series of rulings, decisions, and choices that were favorable to Florida. Consequently, a preliminary finding of sales at less than fair value was made against fresh winter tomatoes from Mexico.

Before the case could be taken to the USITC for an injury determination, *the Mexican tomato growers entered into a "suspension agreement" with the Commerce Department. Under it, Mexican growers promised to always sell their tomatoes above a "reference price" of $5.17 per 25-pound carton.*

As Mr. DiMare testified, *the suspension agreement worked "very, very well" to keep tomato prices up during the first part of this year's season.* Florida growers got high prices for their tomatoes since the Mexican competition was now forced to sell above an artificial price floor.

A problem developed when Florida growers protested price adjustments made for excessive spoilage. The ability to provide for such adjustments is of critical importance to FPAA members who are American distributors for Mexican growers. *FPAA and its members contend and believe that price adjustments for spoilage granted under the provisions of the Perishable Agricultural Products Act (PACA) are legitimate*, and American wholesale buyers of produce are entitled to them, just as they were prior to the suspension agreement.

Mr. DiMare in his testimony alluded to the price adjustment debate and noted that the Commerce Department had not yet come down with a clear ruling which favored the Florida position. In fact, the Commerce Department remains undecided and currently is studying the matter. In the meantime, American consumers may have to accept lower grade tomatoes because of Florida's intransigence.

In winter, the major domestic source of winter vegetables is Florida which has suffered through a series of bad weather conditions for the past two years. Overall, fresh winter vegetables must come from several sources, such as Mexico, since supplies from Florida cannot meet the entire US demand. This season Florida experienced damaging cold weather. *In contrast, Mexico has enjoyed good growing weather during the past several seasons. Cold weather was a factor this year, but Mexico still had enough high quality produce to ship.*

As mentioned earlier, tomato imports from Mexico have increased. *A particularly important factor is the type of tomato shipped from Mexico. Florida tomato growers ship mostly "mature green tomatoes" that are treated with ethylene gas to turn them pink.* Such tomatoes are preferred by restaurant and institutional food operations that like the ease with which the tomatoes can be mechanically sliced.

In contrast, *Mexico ships mostly "vine-ripe tomatoes" which are picked when the tomatoes begin to show color. In recent years, Mexico has shipped an "improved variety" of vine ripe tomatoes which grow especially well in the hot, dry Mexican climate. American consumers have shown preference for the improved variety because the tomatoes stay firm, maintain good color, and taste better than the old variety.*

In looking at the import statistics--whether for tomatoes or manufactured items--attention should be paid to the range of possible reasons for the increase, or decrease, in the level of imports. The raw numbers, without context, can be misleading.

For tomatoes, NAFTA cannot be the reason for increased shipments. Import duties on Mexican tomatoes were not eliminated by NAFTA. In fact, they are being phased out over a ten-year period. The tariff, therefore, is still 70 percent of the original level. Furthermore, the pre-NAFTA tariff rate will apply to tomato imports that exceed the two seasonal tariff-rate quotas that will be in place for ten years.

Furthermore, *tomato imports are subject to Florida's marketing order.* Except for packaging (which is sometimes different to accommodate the more delicate nature of the vine ripe tomatoes from Mexico), all imports meet the grade, quality, and size standards set by the Florida marketing order. Because the majority of Florida tomatoes are mature greens which are very firm (if not hard), the Florida marketing order says the tomatoes should be jumble-packed in 25 lb. cartons. (The small volume of Florida vine ripe tomatoes are not jumble packed in 25-lb. cartons.)

Additionally, *tomato and other vegetable imports meet all FDA regulations,* just like the produce grown in Florida. The rate or frequency of FDA inspection in Nogales, AZ, where the majority of the Mexican winter vegetables enter the US, is especially high, greater than the domestic average.

Tomato imports from Mexico, therefore, have not enjoyed any special or immediate benefits under NAFTA. It is an absolute falsehood to state that NAFTA has given special advantages to Mexican tomatoes or that NAFTA is the direct cause of economic problems for Florida tomato growers.

Agricultural statistics will show that Florida tomato production is down, that acreage has shrunk and that farms are disappearing, going into bankruptcy. *Acreage may be down in Florida, but other states do not show the same decline.* In other words, *if NAFTA is bad for American agriculture, production and acreage should be uniformly down throughout the United States.* Even the agricultural statistics published by the Florida Department of Agriculture show that acreage is up in many instances.

[The Florida winter acreage report published January 21, 1997 by the Florida Agricultural Statistics Service show that 1997 carrot acreage is 107 percent of the 1996 acreage in California, and 131 percent in Florida; for eggplant, the Florida acreage is 117 of last year; for Florida strawberries, 102 percent; for California head lettuce, 103 percent; for

California broccoli, 105 percent, for California cauliflower, 112 percent, and California celery, 108 percent. It should be noted that eggplant, strawberry, broccoli and cauliflower are available from Mexico.]

Florida is not only a desirable place to grow tomatoes, it is obviously a desirable place to live. Residential and commercial development of Florida land is common. Small farm operators retire or quit, and sell to larger farms or land developers. Those are valid reasons why there are fewer tomato farmers today than in the past. Furthermore, farms have become more productive and can produce the same, or greater volume of, tomatoes from fewer acres. That is yet another reason why acreage might be down compared to past years. In addition, the Federal government and the state of Florida have canceled land leases and purchased ecologically sensitive farms from Florida tomato growers to help reduce the environmental damage created by the high chemical input systems used by these farmers. In other words, fewer farms or less acreage do not necessarily tie into NAFTA, and statistics should not be accepted at face value because they are "static" information that do not provide the dynamic fluidity of knowledge and understanding which result from the proper interpretation of data points.

Tomato imports from Mexico may be up, but so are tomato imports from other countries. Admittedly the numbers are small, but *there is a trend towards more internationalization of supply*, and that is not due to NAFTA.

[Commodity shipment and origins reports show tomato imports this season from Belgium, Belize, Israel, Mexico, Netherlands, and Spain. Last year, there were tomato imports from Bahamas, Belgium, Dominican Republic, Israel, Jamaica, Mexico, Netherlands, and Spain. Imported tomatoes do come from many sources.]

US agricultural exports have increased dramatically over the years, and US farm exports consistently show favorable trade balances. Agricultural exports were: 1990, $39.3 billion; 1991, $39.2 billion; 1992, $42.9 billion; 1993, $42.6 billion; 1994, $45.7 billion; 1995, $55.8 billion; and in 1996, $60.4 billion *Favorable trade balances have ranged from $16.5 billion in 1990 to $28.0 billion last year.*

American agriculture is healthy as result of international sales which became increasingly easier with trade liberalization. It is indeed ironic that some American politicians and industrialists would want to attack NAFTA which has helped to increase agricultural sales to Mexico. *Specifically, US agricultural exports to Mexico in 1995 totaled $3.519 billion and in 1996, $5.446 billion. The projection for this year is $5.5 billion.*

Specifically, *US horticultural exports to Mexico have done very well*, except when the peso was devalued. In 1992, horticultural exports totaled $324.5 million; in 1993, $379.7 million, and in 1994, $547.6 million. Unfortunately, with the peso devaluation, exports dropped back to $337.6 million in 1995, but with economic recovery in Mexico, US horticultural exports last year climbed back up to $402.5 million, and apparently is increasing this year again.

Despite such robust agricultural sales to Mexico, overall imports are up so that the US now has a trade deficit. As a result, NAFTA is under fire. *The US runs trade deficits with many countries, but there is not the same obsession or concern about trade deficits with countries other than Mexico.* Italy, for example, has had a trade surplus with the US for years, but there is virtually no talk of retaliating, or withholding MFN, as a means of cutting back imports from Italy.

[US trade deficits with Italy since 1991, according to an USITC report, are as follows: 1991, $3.4 billion, 1992, $3.8 billion, 1993, $6.9 billion, 1994, $7.7 billion, and 1995, $7.9 billion. Also, US trade with the European Union has gone from a surplus to a deficit. USITC says the trade balance was in surplus by $10.7 billion in 1991 and $3.0 billion in 1992. The balance shifted to a deficit in 1993 ($8.4 billion), 1994 ($16.3 billion) , and 1995 ($14.5 billion). Despite these rather dramatic figures, there is little talk of re-arranging our trading relationship with the EU. US trade with Canada also shows imbalance, but there is virtually no protest or objections. *Unfortunately, there is an inordinate amount of concern only when Mexico is involved.*]

NAFTA is an opportunity for the United States. Every bit of economic development in Mexico is an opportunity for more American business, and every financial gain in Mexico is reason for Mexican workers to find jobs in the domestic economy. Every denial of sales to Mexico is another reason for Mexico to deny opportunities for sales by American companies. Every attempt to keep out Mexican goods is another reason for a Mexican worker to seek work here, or for re-enforcing protectionist interests in Mexico.

A very specific benefit of NAFTA has been to move phyto-sanitary disputes to discussions that are more based on science than on politics and economic emotionalism. By basing its decision-making process on science, the US Agriculture Department overcame objections to allowing limited imports of Mexican avocados. For the first time in 90 years, there is a chance that some Hass avocados will be imported. Concurrently, insistence on science has broken the phyto-sanitary regulatory logjam so that US cherry and stonefruit exports are now allowed into Mexico in record numbers. NAFTA, therefore, has helped to bring science into negotiations and that has helped American farm exports.

Trade is inevitably multi-lateral. NAFTA, therefore, conceivably could be disadvantageous to some American companies, since US exports and imports will have to generate a series of pluses and minuses in many countries before the benefits of international trade accrue in each country. *FPAA members have found that the overall effect of NAFTA has been positive for both sales and purchases. FPAA members export considerable amount of goods and services to Mexico.* For example, most of the shipping cartons for tomatoes are made in the US. Tractor parts, tires, agricultural chemicals, and a wide range of inputs are sold to Mexico. As a result, *fresh winter vegetables from Mexico have significant "US content." NAFTA has made those types of trade arrangements possible.* Every indication we see shows that trade between Mexico and the US will grow on that basis.

We see NAFTA, therefore, as a roomful of young students--perhaps a bit of a behavior problem from time to time, but certainly not students that should be suspended or expelled. We see them becoming adults. We will do ourselves disservice and regret our short-sightedness, if we do not help them grow and get strong.

****

A

STATEMENT

ON

THE IMPACT OF THE NORTH AMERICAN FREE TRADE AGREEMENT

ON THE

U.S. ECONOMY AND INDUSTRIES: A THREE-YEAR REVIEW

(INV. NO. 332-381)

TO

THE U.S. INTERNATIONAL TRADE COMMISSION

SUBMITTED BY

WAYNE HAWKINS
EXECUTIVE VICE PRESIDENT

FLORIDA TOMATO EXCHANGE

4401 E. COLONIAL DR.

P.O. BOX 140635

ORLANDO, FL 32814-0635

MAY 15, 1997

U.S. INTERNATIONAL TRADE COMMISSION
(INV. NO. 332-381)
THE IMPACT OF THE NAFTA
ON THE
U.S. ECONOMY AND INDUSTRIES: A THREE-YEAR REVIEW

THURSDAY, MAY 15, 1997

MY NAME IS WAYNE HAWKINS. I AM EXECUTIVE VICE PRESIDENT OF THE FLORIDA TOMATO EXCHANGE, A NON-PROFIT COOPERATIVE AGRICULTURAL ASSOCIATION WHOSE MEMBERS SHIP ABOUT 90 PERCENT OF THE VOLUME OF FRESH TOMATOES FROM FLORIDA EACH YEAR. I AM ALSO MANAGER OF THE FLORIDA TOMATO COMMITTEE WHICH IS THE ADMINISTRATIVE COMMITTEE FOR FEDERAL MARKETING ORDER NO. 966 WHICH REGULATES THE HANDLING OF FRESH TOMATOES SHIPPED IN INTERSTATE COMMERCE FROM THE "PRODUCTION AREA" OF FLORIDA AS DEFINED IN THE ORDER, AND ALSO EXECUTIVE VICE PRESIDENT OF THE FLORIDA TOMATO GROWERS EXCHANGE, A NON-PROFIT COOPERATIVE AGRICULTURAL ASSOCIATION WHOSE MEMBERS ARE TOMATO GROWERS IN CENTRAL AND SOUTH FLORIDA.

TOMATO PRODUCTION IN FLORIDA WAS THE GIANT OF THE VEGETABLE INDUSTRY UNTIL NAFTA WAS IMPLEMENTED. MORE THAN 30 PERCENT OF THE TOTAL VALUE OF ALL VEGETABLES PRODUCED IN FLORIDA CAME FROM FRESH MARKET TOMATOES. THE FARM GATE CROP VALUE FOR TOMATOES FROM 1991-92 TO 1995-96 WAS 643, 569, 428, 388 AND 370 MILLION DOLLARS. THIS IS A REDUCTION OF NEARLY 43 PERCENT IN ONLY FIVE YEARS AND I EXPECT THE 1996-97 SEASON WILL CONTINUE THIS SAME TREND.

DURING THE SAME PERIOD 1991-92 TO 1995-96, IMPORTS OF MEXICAN TOMATOES TO THE U.S. DURING FLORIDA'S SEASON, NOVEMBER THROUGH MAY, HAVE INCREASED 284 PERCENT WITH MANY OF THEM DUMPED ALL OVER THE U.S. AT PRICES THAT DID NOT RETURN THEIR OWN COSTS OF PRODUCTION. FIGURES FOR 1996-97 ARE NOT FINAL, BUT THEY ALSO WILL SHOW A SUBSTANTIAL INCREASE OVER LAST SEASON. THE ONCE VERY PROUD FLORIDA TOMATO INDUSTRY WHICH SUPPLIED MORE THAN 50 PERCENT OF THE DOMESTICALLY GROWN FRESH MARKET TOMATOES IN THE U.S. ANNUALLY AND ABOUT 95 PERCENT DURING MID-DECEMBER TO MID-MAY EACH YEAR HAS BEEN BROUGHT TO ITS KNEES BY UNFAIR COMPETITION FROM MEXICO.

I HAVE BEEN INVOLVED IN THE SO-CALLED FLORIDA/MEXICO TOMATO WAR FOR ABOUT 30 YEARS. I HAVE WATCHED NUMEROUS LAWS PASSED BY THE U.S. GOVERNMENT THAT REGULATED FLORIDA TOMATO GROWERS, BUT EXEMPTED MEXICAN IMPORTS. EVEN WORSE ARE THE LAWS ON THE BOOKS DESIGNED TO REGULATE THE PRODUCTS OF BOTH COUNTRIES BUT MEXICAN IMPORTS ARE EXEMPTED AT THE WHIMS OF BUREAUCRATS WHO TOTALLY IGNORE THE INTENT OF THE LAW.

SECTION 8(E) OF THE AGRICULTURAL MARKETING AGREEMENT ACT REQUIRES IMPORTS TO MEET THE TERMS OR CONDITIONS OF GRADE, SIZE, QUALITY OR MATURITY OF PRODUCTS OPERATING UNDER A FEDERAL MARKETING ORDER. THIS LAW ENACTED IN THE 1950'S AND KNOWN AS THE "GOLDEN RULE" AMENDMENT HAS NEVER BEEN ENFORCED PROPERLY BECAUSE OF BUREAUCRATIC INTERPRETATION. ACCORDING TO THE U.S.D.A., THE WORD "PACK" NEEDS TO BE ADDED TO REQUIRE IMPORTS TO MEET THE SAME SIZE DESIGNATIONS OF TOMATOES IN THE CONTAINER AS THOSE APPLIED TO DOMESTIC PRODUCERS, BUT THEY THEMSELVES ADDED THE WORD "MINIMUM" TO THE TERMS AND CONDITIONS OF THE MARKETING ORDER WHICH TOTALLY CHANGED THE LAW. I HAVE TRIED FOR 30 YEARS OR MORE TO ADD THIS ONE WORD. WHY CAN'T I GET IT CHANGED? WITNESSES AGAINST ME ARE THE DEPARTMENT OF AGRICULTURE, STATE DEPARTMENT, U.S. TRADE REPRESENTATIVE, COMMERCE DEPARTMENT, ETC., ETC. WHAT'S WRONG WITH HAVING IMPORTS PACKED THE SAME AS DOMESTIC PRODUCTS? TOMATOES ARE SOLD BY GRADE, SIZE AND WEIGHT. I DON'T CARE IF THEY ARE PACKED IN SOMBREROS; I JUST WANT TO KNOW WHAT IS IN THE MASTER SHIPPING CONTAINER.

THE U.S. GRADE STANDARDS FOR TOMATOES WERE AMENDED IN 1991 DEFINING MINIMUM AND MAXIMUM DIAMETERS OF EACH SIZE, REQUIRING ONLY ONE SIZE IN A BOX AND REQUIRING THE SIZE TO BE PRINTED ON THE BOX. THIS WOULD HAVE RESOLVED THE PROBLEM DISCUSSED ABOVE. THE DAY THIS AMENDMENT WAS APPROVED, THE U.S.D.A. EXEMPTED MEXICO FROM ABIDING BY THE SIZE REQUIREMENTS DEFINED IN THE U.S. GRADE STANDARDS.

COUNTRY OF ORIGIN LABELLING. IT'S BEEN THE LAW OF THE LAND SINCE 1930, BUT NOT FOR PERISHABLE PRODUCTS. APPARENTLY, IT'S STILL IMPORTANT TO KNOW WHERE YOUR SHIRT OR SHOES WHERE MADE, WHERE YOUR FOUNTAIN PEN WAS MADE, WHERE YOUR KID'S TOYS WERE MADE, BUT IT DOESN'T SEEM TO REALLY MATTER WHERE YOUR FOOD COMES FROM. I GUESS CONGRESS AGREES WITH THIS PREMISE BECAUSE WE CAN'T EVEN GET A HEARING TO DISCUSS THIS LEGISLATION. ANY GOOD TRAVEL AGENCY WILL TELL YOU NOT TO DRINK THE WATER OR EAT ANY FRESH FRUIT OR VEGETABLES IF YOU GO TO MEXICO. WHAT PURIFIES THEM WHEN THEY CROSS THE BORDER?

THESE ARE ONLY A FEW OF THE DUAL STANDARDS. WHAT ABOUT FERTILIZER AND PESTICIDE USE REGULATIONS, THE WORKER'S PROTECTION ACT, MINIMUM WAGE, SOCIAL SECURITY, HEALTH PROTECTION, CHILD LABOR, OSHA -- THE LIST GOES ON AND ON. WHY DOESN'T MEXICAN PRODUCE HAVE TO MEET THE SAME STANDARDS? HOW CAN WE COMPETE WITH PRODUCTS PRODUCED WITH LABORERS WHO ARE PAID LESS PER DAY THAN WE PAY PER HOUR OR WITH CHILD LABOR? FREE TRADE IS FINE, BUT IT MUST BE FAIR TRADE.

KEEP IN MIND -- MEXICAN TOMATOES ARE NOT SOLD FROM MEXICO. THEY ARE CONSIGNED TO RECEIVERS IN NOGALES, ARIZONA; MC ALLEN, TEXAS; SAN DIEGO, CALIFORNIA; AND OTHER U.S. CITIES AND THEN SOLD OR RE-CONSIGNED FROM THERE. WHY DON'T THEY HAVE TO FOLLOW THE U.S. LAWS GOVERNING SALE OF FRESH PRODUCE AT THIS POINT?

THE NUMBER ONE PRODUCTION AREA FOR FRESH TOMATOES SHIPPED TO THE U.S. IS CULIACAN, MEXICO. CULIACAN IS ALSO THE NUMBER ONE ASSEMBLY POINT FOR ILLEGAL DRUGS SHIPPED TO THE U.S. ACCORDING TO THE FEDERAL DRUG AGENCY. WHAT BETTER WAY TO SHIP MARIJUANA, HEROIN OR COCAINE TO THE U.S. THAN BURIED IN A LOAD OF PRODUCE? ESTIMATES OF TRADE IN ILLEGAL DRUGS ARE ESTIMATED AT 20 DOLLARS TO OVER 100 BILLION DOLLARS.

I WAS IN NOGALES, ARIZONA AND MEXICO DURING THE MONTH OF MARCH 1997. TWELVE HUNDRED TO 1,500 TRUCKS WERE CROSSING THE BORDER EVERY DAY. LESS THAN 50 RECEIVED A COMPLETE INSPECTION. THE OTHERS COULD HAVE HAD AN ELEPHANT IN THE NOSE OF THE TRUCK AND NO-ONE WOULD HAVE KNOWN IT. ONLY 25 SAMPLES FOR PESTICIDE RESIDUES WERE TAKEN EACH DAY. WITH ONLY A TWO TO FOUR PERCENT CHANCE OF GETTING CAUGHT AT THE BORDER, THE DETERRENT TO PREVENTING THE USE OF ILLEGAL PESTICIDES OR TO SHIPPING ILLEGAL CONTRABAND TO THE U.S. IS VERY SMALL. THE INSPECTORS DID A GOOD JOB ON THE 40 TO 50 LOADS CHECKED EACH DAY, BUT WHAT ABOUT THE OTHER 1,150 TO 1,450 TRUCKLOADS WHICH RECEIVED ABSOLUTELY NO INSPECTION? WITH SHIPMENTS INCREASING, TENS OF THOUSANDS OF TRUCKLOADS WILL ENTER THE U.S. WITHOUT ANY INSPECTION. WHAT BETTER WAY IS THERE FOR A DRUG LORD TO SEND DRUGS TO AMERICA'S CHILDREN? THE INSPECTION FACILITIES COULD BE ENLARGED AND ALL TRUCKS INSPECTED IF THE POWERS TO BE REALLY WANTED TO STOP CONTRABAND AND CONTAMINATED PRODUCTS COMING TO THE U.S.

THE LAST STRAW AND THE ONE THAT REALLY BROKE THE BACK OF THE FLORIDA TOMATO INDUSTRY WAS THE PASSAGE OF NAFTA. I TESTIFIED BEFORE NUMEROUS COMMITTEES IN WASHINGTON, D.C. AND TOLD THEM WHAT WOULD HAPPEN TO FLORIDA'S PERISHABLE AGRICULTURAL INDUSTRY IF THIS LEGISLATION PASSED. I WAS WRONG! IT'S TEN TIMES WORSE THAN I PREDICTED AND HAPPENED MUCH FASTER THAN I ANTICIPATED. THE DEVALUATION OF THE PESO ERASED ANY ADVANTAGE OF NAFTA FOR AMERICA AND FORCED MEXICO TO INCREASE EXPORTS IN EXCHANGE FOR AMERICAN DOLLARS WHICH ACTUALLY DOUBLED THEIR RETURN. THE FLORIDA TOMATO INDUSTRY WAS PROMISED THAT THEY WOULD BE PROTECTED AND THERE WOULD BE SAFEGUARD PROVISIONS IN NAFTA. UNFORTUNATELY, THE PROMISES MADE WERE NOT KEPT AND THE SAFEGUARD PROVISIONS WERE TRIED BUT DID NOT PROVIDE ANY RELIEF. THE INDUSTRY HAS SUFFERED HUNDREDS OF MILLIONS OF DOLLARS AS A RESULT AND THOUSANDS OF WORKERS HAVE BEEN DISPLACED.

PRIOR TO ANY NEGOTIATIONS ON NAFTA, THE U.S. INTERNATIONAL TRADE COMMISSION (ITC) FOUND THAT THE WINTER VEGETABLE INDUSTRY WAS IN DIRECT COMPETITION WITH MEXICO AND THAT IT WOULD BE NEGATIVELY IMPACTED SHOULD NAFTA BE ADOPTED. IN RESPONSE, OUR TRADE NEGOTIATIONS ADOPTED SEVERAL SAFEGUARD PROVISIONS TO ASSIST OUR INDUSTRY IN TRANSITION TO COMPLETE ELIMINATION OF THE TOMATO TARIFF.

THE FLORIDA TOMATO INDUSTRY RECEIVED A 10-YEAR PHASE OUT OF THE TARIFF. BECAUSE OF THE 40 PERCENT PESO DEVALUATION UNILATERALLY ADOPTED BY THE GOVERNMENT OF MEXICO, IN DECEMBER OF 1994, THIS "BENEFIT" WAS SUBSTANTIALLY, IF NOT TOTALLY, EVISCERATED. NO ACTION WAS TAKEN BY OUR GOVERNMENT TO REPAIR THIS DAMAGE.

THE FLORIDA TOMATO INDUSTRY REQUESTED A PRICE-BASED SAFEGUARD PROVISION WHICH WOULD IMMEDIATELY RESPOND TO DISRUPTIVE CHANGES IN PRICES. INSTEAD, OUR NEGOTIATORS IMPOSED A TARIFF RATE QUOTA (TRQ) SNAP-BACK PROVISION WHICH PROVIDES THAT ONCE A QUOTA IS EXCEEDED DURING THE PERIOD IN QUESTION, THEN THE EXCESS SHIPMENTS WOULD PAY THE MOST FAVORED NATION'S (A HIGHER) TARIFF RATE. DESPITE STARTING WITH A QUOTA FIGURE THAT WAS INAPPROPRIATELY BASED ON A SINGLE, ABNORMAL YEAR, WHICH RESULTED IN THE HIGHEST QUANTITY EVER SHIPPED TO THE U.S., AND WITHOUT NOTICE OR CONSULTATION WITH THE DOMESTIC INDUSTRY, MEXICO HAS EXCEEDED THE QUOTA EACH YEAR OF NAFTA. MORE IMPORTANTLY, THOUGH, BECAUSE THE DATA COLLECTED BY THE U.S. CUSTOMS SERVICE HAS A BUILT-IN DELAY, NOTICE OF THE EXCESSIVE SHIPMENTS HAS NOT INCREASED DUTIES IN A TIMELY FASHION, THEREFORE IT HAD NO AFFECT ON THE PRICES IN THE MARKET PLACE. THIS PROVISION HAD LITTLE OR NO VALUE IN PROTECTING THE INDUSTRY AND EVEN THOUGH FLORIDA COMPLAINED, THERE APPEARS TO BE NO PLANS TO CHANGE THIS PROVISION.

NAFTA'S IMPLEMENTATION STATUTE PROVIDED A SPECIAL PROVISION FOR TOMATO AND PEPPERS ONLY. IT WAS CREATED SOLELY FOR THE BENEFIT OF THE WINTER (FLORIDA) TOMATO AND PEPPER GROWERS. THE PROVISION AUTHORIZED THE ITC TO BEGIN THE PROCESS OF COLLECTING INFORMATION IN ADVANCE ON THESE COMMODITIES SO THAT EITHER COULD BRING AN IMMEDIATE (CALLED PROVISIONAL RELIEF) ACTION TO THE ITC WHICH IS REQUIRED TO PROVIDE A DECISION WITHIN A SEVERAL WEEK TIME PERIOD.

THE FLORIDA TOMATO INDUSTRY TRIED AN ACTION UNDER THIS PROVISION AND LOST IN SUBSTANTIAL PART BECAUSE THE ITC DID NOT RECOGNIZE THAT THIS REMEDY INCLUDED ONLY THE FLORIDA TOMATO INDUSTRY AS NEGOTIATED IN NAFTA. DESPITE LEGISLATIVE ACTION TO CHANGE THIS PROVISION FOR TOMATOES AND PEPPERS WITH THE SUPPORT OF THE ADMINISTRATION THE BILL DID NOT PASS. HOWEVER, ACTION TAKEN UNDER THE PRESENT SUSPENSION AGREEMENT BETWEEN THE U.S. COMMERCE DEPARTMENT AND THE MEXICAN GROWERS DID POINT OUT A REAL COST OF PRODUCTION DIFFERENCE BETWEEN CULIACAN AND BAJA, MEXICO AND FLORIDA AND CALIFORNIA PRODUCERS.

PRESIDENT CLINTON IN A LAST MINUTE EFFORT TO GAIN SUPPORT FOR NAFTA FROM A BLOCK OF THE FLORIDA DELEGATION STATED IN A LETTER TO REPRESENTATIVE TOM LEWIS, "I AM COMMITTED TO TAKE THE NECESSARY STEPS TO INSURE THAT THE U.S.T.R. AND THE I.T.C. TAKE PROMPT AND EFFECTIVE ACTION TO PROTECT THE U.S. VEGETABLE INDUSTRY AGAINST PRICE-BASED IMPORT SURGES FROM MEXICO." (COPY OF LETTER ATTACHED.) THIS OFFER WAS MADE TO GET FLORIDA VOTES FOR NAFTA. HE OFFERED THE FULL MOON OVER THE PASTURE. HE GOT HIS VOTES. THE FLORIDA VEGETABLE INDUSTRY GOT THE COW PATTIES IN THE PASTURE.

EFFORTS TO OBTAIN RELIEF FROM UNFAIR MEXICAN COMPETITION WERE FILED BY THE FLORIDA TOMATO INDUSTRY UNDER SECTIONS 201 AND 202 OF THE TRADE LAW OF 1974 AND UNDER PROVISIONS OF THE ANTI-DUMPING LAWS OF THE U.S.

EVIDENCE PRESENTED TO THE ITC IN THE SECTION 201 AND 202 CASES IN 1995 AND 1996 DOCUMENTED 24 PACKINGHOUSES AND MORE THAN 100 TOMATO GROWERS THAT HAD GONE OUT OF BUSINESS SINCE 1990-91. THE ITC ACCEPTED THESE FACTS, BUT FOUR OF THE FIVE VOTING COMMISSIONERS STILL VOTED THAT THE EVIDENCE DID NOT SUPPORT THE PREMISE THAT MEXICAN IMPORTS WERE A SUBSTANTIAL CAUSE OF SERIOUS INJURY OR THREAT THEREOF TO THE DOMESTIC INDUSTRIES PRODUCING TOMATOES IN THE U.S. A LETTER SENT TO CHAIRMAN OF THE ITC ROHR ASKING FOR A DEFINITION OF SERIOUS INJURY AND MATERIAL INJURY WAS NEVER ANSWERED. WHAT DO THOSE TERMS MEAN? I WONDER IF ANYONE REALLY KNOWS!!

THE ONE COMMISSIONER, LYNN BRAGG, WHO VOTED IN FLORIDA'S FAVOR STATED, "IN MY VIEW, BY MAKING A NEGATIVE DETERMINATION IN THESE INVESTIGATIONS THE COMMISSION MAJORITY HAS SET A STANDARD FOR OBTAINING RELIEF UNDER SECTION 201 THAT IS VIRTUALLY IMPOSSIBLE TO SATISFY." THIS IS CERTAINLY VERIFIED IN THE FACT THAT ONLY TWO 201 CASES HAVE BEEN WON BY THE PETITIONERS BEFORE THE ITC SINCE 1986.

THIS AGAIN POINTS OUT THAT THE SAFEGUARD PROVISIONS UNDER NAFTA AND OUR OTHER TRADE LAWS DO NOT WORK FOR PERISHABLE AGRICULTURAL COMMODITIES. THERE ARE NO PROVISIONS FOR SEASONAL RELIEF, IT MUST COVER THE ENTIRE U.S. INDUSTRY FOR THE WHOLE YEAR. A 90-DAY TOMATO CROP IS CERTAINLY A SEASONAL PROBLEM AND MAY OR MAY NOT AFFECT CROPS IN OTHER GROWING AREAS. EFFORTS TO AMEND THIS LAW HAVE BEEN FUTILE. THE AMENDMENTS PASSED THE SENATE BUT WERE THEN CHALLENGED BY ONE SENATOR AND SENT BACK TO THE SENATE FOR RECONSIDERATION. A HEARING WAS HELD BEFORE THE TRADE SUBCOMMITTEE OF THE HOUSE WAYS AND MEANS COMMITTEE. HOWEVER, NO VOTE WAS EVER TAKEN.

THE U.S. COMMERCE DEPARTMENT ISSUED A PRELIMINARY FINDING UNDER THE ANTI-DUMPING CASE THAT INDICATED MEXICO HAD DUMPED TOMATOES INTO THE U.S. AT LESS THAN FAIR VALUE. FOLLOWING A RECOMMENDATION BY THE COMMERCE DEPARTMENT, THE FLORIDA TOMATO INDUSTRY AGREED TO ACCEPT THE TERMS ESTABLISHED UNDER A SUSPENSION AGREEMENT BETWEEN MEXICAN TOMATO GROWERS AND THE COMMERCE DEPARTMENT THAT ESTABLISHED A FLOOR PRICE ON IMPORTS OF MEXICAN TOMATOES. THIS APPEARED TO BE A SOLUTION TO THE PROBLEM AND WORKED WELL IN THE BEGINNING.

CHANGES IN THE ENFORCEMENT OF THE SUSPENSION AGREEMENT BY THE COMMERCE DEPARTMENT MONTHS AFTER IT WAS APPROVED AND CONTRARY TO THE EXPRESS LANGUAGE IN THE AGREEMENT WILL UNDOUBTEDLY WEAKEN THE EFFECTIVENESS OF THE AGREEMENT. THE MEXICAN GROWERS ALSO ASKED THE U.S. TO CONSIDER RAISING THE MINIMUM GRADE STANDARDS ON TOMATOES IMPORTED INTO THE U.S. WHICH WOULD HAVE HELPED GROWERS BOTH HERE AND IN MEXICO, BUT THE U.S. JUSTICE DEPARTMENT TORPEDOED THIS IDEA. ONCE AGAIN, IT APPEARS THAT THE U.S. GOVERNMENT WILL CONTINUE TO MAKE INTERPRETATIONS OF THE AGREEMENT THAT FAVOR THE MEXICAN POSITION AND ARE DETRIMENTAL TO THE U.S. TOMATO INDUSTRY.

IN 1974 WHEN I BECAME MANAGER OF THE FLORIDA TOMATO COMMITTEE THERE WERE 475 TOMATO GROWERS ON THE MAILING LIST. IN 1990-91 THERE WERE 230 AND TODAY THERE ARE LESS THAN 75. DROPS IN NUMBERS OF PRODUCERS FOR EACH OF THE OTHER WINTER VEGETABLES ARE SIMILAR. THIS CLEARLY SHOWS WHAT NAFTA HAS DONE FOR FLORIDA AGRICULTURE. IT LOOKS LIKE IT WILL BE THE KISS-OF-DEATH FOR FLORIDA VEGETABLE PRODUCTION.

ACCORDING TO ARTICLES RECENTLY APPEARING IN SEVERAL MAJOR NEWSPAPERS MANY OTHER INDUSTRIES ARE APPARENTLY NOT FARING TOO WELL EITHER. THE L.A. TIMES SYNDICATED APRIL 25, 1997, REPORTED, "BOOSTERS, INCLUDING THE PRESIDENT, PREDICTED THAT NAFTA WOULD CREATE 200,000 HIGH-PAYING JOBS FOR AMERICAN WORKERS. INSTEAD, USING THE COMMERCE DEPARTMENT'S FORMULA, AS MANY AS 600,000 JOBS MAY HAVE BEEN DESTROYED AS U.S. FACTORIES FLED TO MEXICO.

"DEMOCRATIC REP. DAVID BONIOR OF MICHIGAN - ONE OF THE DWINDLING BREED OF CONGRESSMEN WHO STILL GOES OUT ON SOLIDARITY MARCHES WITH MIGRANT FARM WORKERS - REPORTS, 'TIJUANA NOW PRODUCES MORE TELEVISIONS THAN ANY PLACE IN THE WORLD ... INSTEAD OF SELLING OUR TV'S TO MEXICO, WE ARE NOW BUYING THEM FROM MEXICO. THOUSANDS OF JOBS HAVE BEEN LOST IN THIS SECTOR.'

"DEMOCRATIC REP. PETER DEFAZIO OF OREGON WAS PROMISED THAT HIS STATE, WITH ITS NEW HIGH-TECHNOLOGY INDUSTRIES, WOULD BE ONE OF THE WINNERS FROM NAFTA. INSTEAD, HE SAID, IT RANKS FIFTH IN THE

NATION IN JOB LOSSES ATTRIBUTABLE TO FREE TRADE WITH MEXICO. 'THIS AGREEMENT WAS NEVER INTENDED TO CREATE A MARKET FOR AMERICAN PRODUCTS,' DEFAZIO SAID. 'THIS AGREEMENT WAS ALWAYS ABOUT PROTECTING THE MOVEMENT OF U.S. CAPITAL AND MANUFACTURING RESOURCES TO MEXICO TO EXPLOIT THE CHEAP LABOR, THE LACK OF ENFORCEMENT OF SAFETY STANDARDS AND THE LACK OF ENFORCEMENT OF ENVIRONMENTAL LAWS.'

"GLOBAL TRADE WATCH, ONE OF RALPH NADER'S PUBLIC-INTEREST GROUPS, REPORTS THAT GENERAL ELECTRIC, WHICH PROMISED 10,000 NEW JOBS, IN FACT LAID OFF 2,254 BY SHIFTING PRODUCTION TO MEXICO. MATTEL, THE TOY MAKER, TALKED OF 2,000 JOBS; IT LAID OFF 520 PEOPLE BECAUSE OF IMPORTS FROM MEXICO.

"FREE TRADE INDEED HAS ITS BENEFITS. IF NAFTA IS EXPANDED, U.S. BANKS MIGHT BE ABLE TO OPERATE FREELY IN CHILE. CHEAP IMPORTS HOLD DOWN CONSUMER PRICES. BUT THERE ARE ALSO COSTS - TO JOBS, TO WAGES AND TO COMMUNITIES DEVASTATED WHEN A MAIN INDUSTRY MOVES SOUTH OF THE BORDER."

ACCORDING TO DEPARTMENT OF COMMERCE FIGURES, THE U.S. TRADE DEFICIT HAS WORSENED IN EACH YEAR OF NAFTA. IN 1992, THE TRADE DEFICIT WAS 84.5 BILLION DOLLARS; IN 1993 WAS 111.5 BILLION DOLLARS; IN 1994 WAS 150 BILLION DOLLARS; IN 1995 WAS 158 BILLION DOLLARS; AND IN 1996 WAS 166 BILLION DOLLARS.

AT THE TIME OF PASSAGE NAFTA WAS CONTROVERSIAL AND REMAINS SO TODAY. THE AGREEMENT UNDOUBTEDLY INCREASED TRADE AND INVESTMENT AMONG THE THREE COUNTRIES AND PARTICULARLY BETWEEN THE U.S. AND MEXICO. THE VOLUME OF TRADE HAS INCREASED CONSIDERABLY. EXPORTS TO MEXICO FROM THE U.S. HAVE RISEN FROM 41 BILLION DOLLARS IN 1993 TO 56 BILLION IN 1996. CONVERSELY, IMPORTS FROM MEXICO HAVE RISEN FROM 40 BILLION DOLLARS IN 1994 TO 72 BILLION DOLLARS IN 1996.

THIS HAS CREATED AN ENORMOUS TRADE DEFICIT WITH MEXICO WHICH WAS NOT PRESENT PRIOR TO NAFTA. FOR THE THREE YEARS BEFORE THE AGREEMENT WENT INTO EFFECT, THE U.S. TRADE BALANCE WITH MEXICO WAS A SURPLUS OF BETWEEN ONE AND FIVE BILLION DOLLARS. SINCE NAFTA HAS BEEN IN EFFECT, THE BALANCE HAS DEGRADED FROM A SURPLUS OF 1.3 BILLION DOLLARS IN 1994 TO DEFICITS IN 1995 AND 1996 OF 15.3 AND 16.2 BILLION DOLLARS, RESPECTIVELY. THE U.S. TRADE DEFICIT WITH CANADA IN 1996 WAS 22.8 BILLION DOLLARS.

THE ADMINISTRATION'S SUPPORT OF THE AGREEMENT FOCUSES PRIMARILY ON THE INCREASE IN EXPORTS TO MEXICO. THE ADMINISTRATION NOTES THAT U.S. EXPORTS ACCOUNT FOR APPROXIMATELY THREE-FOURTHS OF ALL MEXICAN IMPORTS. THEY ALSO ARGUE THAT BECAUSE OF NAFTA, MEXICO DID NOT RAISE TARIFFS ON IMPORTED PRODUCTS DURING THE PESO DEVALUATION CRISIS.

OPPONENTS OF NAFTA FOCUS ON THE TRADE DEFICIT AND THE NATURE OF IMPORTS TO MEXICO AND EXPORTS FROM MEXICO. OF PARTICULAR CONCERN IS THE AUTOMOBILE TRADE DEFICIT. ALTHOUGH THERE IS SOME DISCREPANCY ON THE EXACT FIGURES, CONSERVATIVE ESTIMATES PLACE THE U.S.-MEXICO TRADE DEFICIT AT MORE THAN 500,000 CARS. ACCORDING TO THE INTERNATIONAL TRADE COMMISSION THE U.S. IMPORTED 550,622 CARS FROM MEXICO IN 1996 AND SOLD ONLY 46,652 CARS THERE. THE TRUCK DEFICIT IS SIMILAR, WITH IMPORTS OF 198,541 AND EXPORTS OF 30,871. MOREOVER, THE PARTS DEFICITS WITH MEXICO IS SIGNIFICANT AS WELL, APPROXIMATELY 4.5 BILLION DOLLARS IN 1996. IT IS THE PARTS DEFICIT THAT DIFFERENTIATES THE NATURE OF THE DEFICIT WITH MEXICO FROM CANADA. ALTHOUGH THE U.S. HAS A SIGNIFICANT MOTOR VEHICLE DEFICIT WITH CANADA (21 BILLION DOLLARS IN 1996), THE U.S. MAINTAINS A TRADE SURPLUS IN THE PARTS AREA (9.5 BILLION IN 1996).

AS OF APRIL, THE DEPARTMENT OF LABOR HAS CERTIFIED 116,418 WORKERS AS HAVING LOST THEIR JOBS AS A RESULT OF NAFTA. HOWEVER, THIS IS GENERALLY CONCEDED TO COVER ONLY NARROW CATEGORIES. ESTIMATES OF ACTUAL JOB LOSS ARE CLOSER TO 600,000. MOREOVER, SEVERAL MULTINATIONAL COMPANIES WHICH PROMISED TO CREATE JOBS AS A RESULT OF NAFTA (ALLIED SIGNAL, G.E., PROCTOR & GAMBLE, MATTEL, SCOTT PAPER AND ZENITH) HAVE ALL LAID OFF WORKERS AS A RESULT OF NAFTA (AS CERTIFIED BY THE DEPARTMENT OF LABOR).

AN IMPORTANT LESSON CAN BE LEARNED FROM STUDYING THE RESULTS OF ONLY THREE YEARS OF NAFTA. IT MAY WORK FOR SOME INDUSTRIES, BUT OVERALL IT HAS BEEN A DISASTER. IF CONTINUED AND EXPANDED AS IS PRESENTLY PLANNED, IT COULD BE THE START OF HARD TIMES FOR MANY U.S. CITIZENS. GOOD PAYING JOBS WILL BE REPLACED BY MINIMUM WAGE JOBS AND THE STANDARD OF LIVING IN THE GOOD OLD U.S.A. WILL BE LOWERED.

BEFORE CONSIDERING FAST TRACK APPROVAL OF MORE NAFTA TRADE AGREEMENTS, LET'S FIX THE ONE WE NOW HAVE OR GET RID OF IT. WHY LEGISLATE THE END OF IMPORTANT INDUSTRIES LIKE THE FLORIDA TOMATO INDUSTRY AND DISPLACE THOUSANDS OF WORKERS? MAYBE IF MORE LEGISLATORS HAD TO MEET PAYROLLS EACH WEEK, IT WOULD PLACE A DIFFERENT PERSPECTIVE ON THE SITUATION.

THE WHITE HOUSE

WASHINGTON

November 16, 1993

Dear Tom:

I know you have been a leader in assuring that under NAFTA our fresh vegetable industry is not adversely affected by unforeseen price changes. I strongly believe that the volume-based snapback of the existing agreement, coupled with the automatic price monitoring and the expedited import relief procedure which will be the law after NAFTA is passed will provide very effective price and volume discipline.

I am committed to take the necessary steps to ensure that the USTR and the ITC take prompt and effective action to protect the U.S. vegetable industry against price based import surges from Mexico.

I want you to know that I am personally committed to ensuring that this system is enforceable and effective. It will work to ensure against unfair pricing by importers.

Sincerely,

Bill

The Honorable Tom Lewis
House of Representatives
Washington, D.C. 20515

TRANSPORTATION TRADES DEPARTMENT AFL-CIO

TTD

STATEMENT OF
EDWARD WYTKIND, EXECUTIVE DIRECTOR
TRANSPORTATION TRADES DEPARTMENT, AFL-CIO

BEFORE THE
COMMITTEE ON INTERNATIONAL RELATIONS
SUBCOMMITTEE ON INTERNATIONAL ECONOMIC POLICY AND TRADE

"Report Card on NAFTA"
March 5, 1997

Submitted April 4, 1997

The Transportation Trades Department, AFL-CIO (TTD), whose affiliated unions represent several million workers employed in the aviation, aerospace, highway, rail, transit, trucking and related industries, is pleased to submit comments to the House Committee on International Relations, Subcommittee on International Economic Policy and Trade for a hearing held on Wednesday, March 5, 1997, entitled "A Report Card on NAFTA." Attached for your interest is a list of TTD's affiliates.

At the outset, we would like to associate ourselves with the oral and written comments of Ron Carey, president of the International Brotherhood of Teamsters and our organization, who presented testimony to this committee on March 5, 1997.

It is our view that NAFTA has not lived up to the expectations of its proponents and more danger lies in the immediate future as a result of the agreement. Serious deficiencies in the agreement have afforded Mexico a comparative advantage over the U.S. by maintaining low wages and weak environmental, health and safety standards. By 1996, our trade surplus with Mexico

400 N. Capitol Street, NW, Suite 861
Washington, DC 20001
phone 202.628.9262 . fax 202.628.0391

Ron Carey, President
Sonny Hall, Secretary-Treasurer
Edward Wytkind, Executive Director

evaporated and was replaced by a $16.3 billion trade deficit, the largest ever with Mexico, resulting in the loss of thousands of U.S. jobs. The Department of Labor's statistics support the conclusion that jobs are being lost in record numbers, with approximately 110,000 workers qualifying for job re-training or extended unemployment benefits under NAFTA's Transitional Adjustment Assistance (TAA) program. Even more troubling is the fact that the TAA number vastly understates the degree of NAFTA-related job loss. The program covers only certain workers in certain industries, excludes transportation workers entirely, and many workers simply do not apply to the program or meet its strict criteria.

Aside from the macroeconomic and job-impact issues related to NAFTA, there are significant issues which remain unaddressed regarding the opening of the U.S.-Mexico border to commercial traffic, an action which was suspended in December 1995. Fourteen months ago, the Clinton Administration wisely postponed the land transportation provisions of NAFTA. These provisions, among other things, would provide Mexican commercial vehicles with full access to the four border states — Texas, New Mexico, Arizona, and California. In the year 2000, all restrictions would be lifted and Mexican motor carriers would be granted full access to the United States. To prepare for the border opening, the Department of Transportation (DOT), along with other executive branch agencies and their Mexican counterparts, have attempted to harmonize rules and regulations to the best degree possible. Efforts have been made to provide adequate border inspection capabilities which would protect American workers, travelers and highway users from under-qualified drivers and substandard equipment and vehicles.

Unfortunately, the Clinton Administration has not made sufficient progress on these fronts, and many of the problems that were present 14 months ago remain. It is clear that opening the border at this time is dangerously premature and will result in an unsafe situation on our nation's highways and will unnecessarily threaten good U.S. jobs.

First, border inspection capabilities are inadequate. The current level of enforcement personnel allows for the inspection of only one-half of one percent of all trucks crossing the border. The GAO has found that 1 in 200 trucks entering the United States at Laredo, Texas, the busiest crossing, is inspected. Of those that are inspected, ½ are ordered out of service for such serious safety violations as bald tires, cracked frames, missing lug nuts, unqualified drivers, and inadequate or false insurance. Texas alone had 1.9 million total truck crossings in 1995 at 15 different border crossing sites and while complete data is not yet available, it is expected that traffic is on the rise and will only increase.

In view of these amazing deficiencies, declarations that foreign carriers must comply with U.S. laws are meaningless without competent oversight and agreement on comprehensive standards. Despite border state commitments to increase oversight, the number of trained truck inspectors on duty at the border has increased insignificantly.

The end result is that safety on our nation's highways is seriously jeopardized. For example, the area of hazardous material transportation is particularly illustrative. Approximately 1 in 4, or 25 percent of Mexican trucks entering the United States carry hazardous materials. When a random inspection does occur, it was found that less than 1 in 14 of the trucks carrying hazardous materials is properly placarded and up to 90 percent of inspected hazardous materials shipments don't coincide with shipping papers carried by the driver.

A second set of issues deals with the qualifications of Mexican drivers and the integrity of their equipment. Currently, Mexican drivers are not required to comply with U.S. safety and driver standards such as drug and alcohol regulations and hours of service regulations. Mexican drivers do not log their hours of driving and rest while their U.S. counterparts must account for three full days before driving a truck and then cannot drive more than 10 hours per day. Even if hours of service regulations were promulgated and adopted in Mexico, there is absolutely no track record for enforcing such regulations. The entire burden would fall on U.S. officials who are already understaffed and do not have the resources to put a credible enforcement program in place. We cannot allow unqualified and inadequately regulated Mexican drivers, who may be sleep deprived or in violation of numerous U.S. laws, including drug and alcohol regulations, to have unlimited access to our highways.

A related problem is a lack of adequate insurance. Studies conducted by the National Association of Independent Insurers and other interested groups have shown that Mexican motor carriers are chronically under-insured. Oftentimes the legitimacy of insurance papers are questionable and insurance forms are often altered or duplicated. Inadequate or illegitimate policies can be purchased for $50 or less at many border crossing locations. This puts American workers and companies who are complying with insurance requirements at a competitive disadvantage. It also creates the very real possibility that injured Americans may not be able to receive just compensation for incidents involving Mexican motor carriers.

Thirdly, resources do not exist to ensure that Mexican drivers are protected by appropriate U.S. laws and regulations governing worker standards. With the proposed border opening Mexican drivers could work full-time in this country, but not enjoy the protections that their U.S. counterparts receive such as the minimum wage. This creates a very threatening situation for American workers who will see their jobs taken by employees who work longer hours with far less pay. NAFTA's impact on workers' wages and job security is already severe. Opening the border under this circumstance would only increase the harm to U.S. workers by undermining legally mandated wages and other standards.

A fourth set of issues deals with the implications of Mexican passenger bus operations running point-to-point service within the United States, which constitutes cabotage and is an apparent violation of NAFTA. There are arguably illegal operations being conducted by Mexican bus companies within the United States and there is a legitimate concern that some of the largest Mexican bus companies are not complying with Federal Highway Administration safety and insurance requirements. For example, Valley Transit Company, a small, family-owned bus company headquartered in Harlingen, Texas, has documented instances where Mexican bus companies are running over their routes in violation of NAFTA, and has lost some charters that are wholly within the U.S. due to this practice. Not only are the Mexican carriers operating in apparent violation of NAFTA, but they are doing so in an unsafe manner. It was later discovered that the Mexican carrier involved in one particular incident was traveling with $1,000,000 of insurance, rather than the $5,000,000 which is required to operate within the United States.

The economic advantages enjoyed by the Mexican bus industry attributable to lower labor costs and costs associated with regulatory compliance threatens the much smaller U.S. bus companies and their employees which must compete with Mexican bus operators in the border states. U.S. bus companies pay higher wages, higher insurance costs, and must comply with drug and alcohol testing and other federal mandates. It is simply inconceivable that a company like Valley Transit, which pays its drivers over $11 per hour, can compete with Mexican drivers who are paid less than that for driving all day. In fact, many Mexican workers earn less than a dollar an hour.

On a separate issue, despite assertions to the contrary, Mexico has not established reciprocal market access for scheduled bus service originating in the U.S. Mexico continues to restrict service to multiple destinations and prohibits bus terminal ownership and operation by non-Mexican companies, thereby effectively denying market access to U.S. carriers. Until these iniquities are addressed, it is not fair to grant Mexican bus companies further rights to operate in the United States where they will deprive U.S. citizens of much needed employment. Attached please find Comments of the Transportation Trades Department, AFL-CIO to the Interstate Commerce Commission [No. Ex Parte 37 (Sub No. 43)], dated October 24, 1994, which further illustrates these concerns in the proposed commercial zone for McAllen, Texas. In this instance, spot-checks of buses entering from Mexico revealed fraudulent insurance, and demonstrate total disregard for the law and public safety.

We congratulate the Committee on International Relations for conducting oversight hearings on the effects of NAFTA, and appreciate the opportunity to present our views. We look forward to working with the Committee in the future to continue this dialogue.

TTD AFFILIATES

The following labor organizations are members of and represented by the TTD:

Air Line Pilots Association
Amalgamated Transit Union
American Federation of State, County and Municipal Employees
American Federation of Teachers
Association of Flight Attendants
American Train Dispatchers Department
Brotherhood of Locomotive Engineers
Brotherhood of Maintenance of Way Employes
Brotherhood of Railroad Signalmen
Communications Workers of America
Hotel Employees and Restaurant Employees Union
International Association of Fire Fighters
International Association of Machinists and Aerospace Workers
International Brotherhood of Boilermakers, Blacksmiths, Forgers and Helpers
International Brotherhood of Electrical Workers
International Brotherhood of Teamsters
International Longshoremen's and Warehousemen's Union
International Union of Operating Engineers
Marine Engineers Beneficial Association
Professional Airways Systems Specialists
Retail, Wholesale and Department Store Union
Service Employees International Union
Sheet Metal Workers International Association
Transportation • Communications International Union
Transport Workers Union of America
United Brotherhood of Carpenters and Joiners of America
United Mine Workers of America
United Steelworkers of America
United Transportation Union

January 10, 199"

TRANSPORTATION TRADES DEPARTMENT AFL-CIO

BEFORE THE
INTERSTATE COMMERCE COMMISSION
WASHINGTON, D.C.

No. Ex Parte 37 (Sub No. 43)

McAllen, TX Commercial Zone -- Passenger Operations

COMMENTS OF THE
TRANSPORTATION TRADES DEPARTMENT, AFL-CIO

October 24, 1994

The Transportation Trades Department, AFL-CIO ("TTD"), on behalf of its 30 affiliated unions, files these Comments supporting the redefinition of the McAllen commercial zone for passenger carriers. These comments are in response to the Decision of the Interstate Commerce Commission served August 22, 1994 and published in the *Federal Register* on August 23, 1994. Attached please find a list of TTD's affiliates.

Proposed Commercial Zone for McAllen, Texas

§ 1048.20. McAllen, Texas.

The zone adjacent to, and commercially a part of McAllen, Texas, within which transportation by motor carriers of passengers in regular-route service is partially exempt from regulation under 49 U.S.C. 10526(b)(1) shall be deemed to consist of (i) all territory within the corporate limits of McAllen, Texas; (ii) all unincorporated areas within 6 miles of its corporate limits; (iii) all of any other municipality any part of which is within 6 miles of the corporate limits of

400 N. Capitol Street, NW, suite 861
Washington, DC 20001
phone 202.628.9262
fax 202.628.0391

Ron Carey
President
G. Thomas DuBose
Secretary-Treasurer

of its corporate limits; (iii) all of any other municipality any part of which is within 6 miles of the corporate limits of McAllen, provided that the motor carrier operating any route in such zone also is lawfully providing intrastate transportation of passengers over the entire route.

Background

TTD has been closely following developments along the International Boundary between the United States and Mexico following enactment of the North American Free Trade Agreement ("NAFTA"). In particular, TTD is interested in those matters which may have a detrimental impact on the financial health of transportation carriers, safety, and the security of tens of thousands of jobs in a work force already reeling from destructive regulatory policies.

After considering the initial presentation of the City of McAllen, Valley Transit Company, Inc. ("Valley Transit"), the Railroad Commission of Texas ("RCT") and the Attorney General of Texas, TTD has concluded that the positions expressed therein warrant serious consideration. The results of the recent survey that is described in the October 10 filing of the RCT in this docket have confirmed the belief that affirmative steps must be taken at this time in order to forestall serious safety and economic consequences.

At the outset, TTD must acknowledge that it has no way to develop information that would permit it to compare the operations of the exempt foreign carriers and regulated carriers. Given the findings of the RCT that are based on a one-day survey, TTD feels the Commission and the U.S. Department of Transportation should jointly conduct their own investigation to ascertain whether the survey results are indicative of standard operating procedures among the exempt foreign carriers.

Further, throughout the debate over NAFTA, prior to and following its approval by Congress, it has been the view of transportation labor that the freer flow of cross-border trade resulting from NAFTA will pave the way for a flood of low-wage, poorly regulated motor carriers (truck and bus) at a time when safety on our highways already poses significant challenges to federal, state and local enforcement authorities.

When the results of the RCT survey are matched against the numerous Commission enforcement proceedings over the past two years involving illegal Mexican passenger carriers and the investigative reports published in press accounts detailing the many violations of insurance and hours of service regulations, it is abundantly clear that a major problem exists in South Texas that is not going away. And these problems serve as a perfect illustration of what to expect across the nation when NAFTA enters into full force.

As referenced above, TTD actively participated in the NAFTA debate because of the immense impact this flawed trade agreement will have on transportation employees. During the course of the Congressional debates, TTD was able to provide Congress with certain economic data contrasting the wage differential between Mexican drivers and U.S. drivers. That data, obtained from the Harlingen, Texas Chamber of Commerce, illustrates that Mexican drivers earn as little as the equivalent of $9 per day. While wages in the Mexican trucking and bus sectors vary, it is widely accepted that U.S. driver wages exceed Mexico driver wages by at least four times (under the best of conditions), not counting benefits such as health care and pensions. Valley Transit drivers, on the other hand, earn approximately $11 per hour.

It was largely because of this vast disparity in wages that the U.S. negotiators were compelled to negotiate a staggered schedule of entry for Mexican regular-route bus operators. Had the Mexican bus companies been authorized to enter the border States immediately after NAFTA's enactment, many medium and small size U.S. carriers would have been destroyed or forced to downsize immediately due to such a significant financial disadvantage.

In case the Commission is not aware of it, there are several Mexican bus companies which are much larger than Greyhound in terms of the number of buses operated. As such, a small carrier such as Valley Transit with less than 100 buses would have been driven from the market place by the lower-cost Mexican bus operators, primarily because Valley Transit could not match the much lower wage-scale paid by the Mexican carriers. That, in turn, would have left many of the smaller communities in the Rio Grande Valley and South Texas without any scheduled, regular-route bus service, in addition to significant job dislocation.

TTD further requests the Commission to carefully note that while the ICC has provided bus and van operators with more border access to the border communities in the U.S. than is available to bus operators elsewhere, Mexico has <u>not</u> reciprocated. It was the lack of reciprocity that caused Congress to enact the moratorium in 1982. While Canada quickly responded, thereby allowing the President to lift the moratorium against Canada, Mexico continued to reserve its commerce for its own nationals.

The only breakthrough has been in the area of charter and tour operations. While Mexico has agreed to allow U.S. tour and charter operators to operate within Mexico, it has refused to retreat from its near absolute refusal to allow for-hire passenger operations on regular-route operations. As such, the playing field remains heavily tilted in favor of the Mexican carriers which today are operating regular-route operations into the border communities and beyond at the expense of U.S. companies and their workers.

The Commission has also invited comments concerning its jurisdiction to deal with the problem. As reflected by 49 U.S.C. § 10526, the Commission has jurisdiction over transportation in commercial zones when the Commission finds it necessary "to carry out the transportation policy of section 10101." TTD submits that this is a classic situation where the wages and working conditions of American citizens and taxpayers are being threatened by the unfettered ability of foreign operators to penetrate the American marketplace to divert passengers from regulated American operators. This is an area over which the ICC must aggressively assert jurisdiction as it readies itself to deal with the onslaught of Mexican carriers when NAFTA enters into full force.

TTD also submits that the needs of passengers and highway users include the ability to rely on the fact that the carrier has adequate insurance. As the RCT survey indicates, the Mexican carriers are not complying with that basic requirement. The fact that they have provided bus drivers with phony insurance papers reflects not only an undeniable awareness of the regulations, but an obvious indifference to compliance with U.S. laws and regulations.

While the RCT survey was reflective of only one day, there is nothing to indicate that the problem is not widespread. Furthermore, given the press reports indicating that most illegal operations are conducted on the weekends and at night, the survey obviously represents only the tip of the iceberg.

Moreover, this is just the beginning of a long-term problem. If the Commission and DOT are not able to deal effectively with the illegal bus and van operators who are already entering the regular-route passenger market, how can they expect to deal with the flood of Mexican carriers, truck and bus, which will be allowed to enter the marketplace in two years under NAFTA?

It should also be noted that the Commission has jurisdiction over vehicles, such as vans, which are operated on a regular route or between specified places. 49 U.S.C. § 10526(a)(2). The vans used on travel between Reynosa and Monterrey, on the one hand, and McAllen, Houston and other points in Texas via the multiple border communities, are clearly operating under the Commission's and DOT's jurisdiction.

As such, the drivers should meet the same standards as U.S. drivers, should be subjected to the same drug and alcohol tests, and should be required to maintain proper logs reflecting hours of service. These requirements have been enacted not to protect the drivers, but rather to protect the passengers who have entrusted their lives to the drivers and the companies for whom they work. Given this undeniable regulatory purpose, the

Commission should recognize that by taking steps to eliminate the exempt operators, who are not in compliance with the safety standards that are rigorously enforced in other parts of the country, the Commission is penalizing the regulated carriers who are bearing the full cost of regulatory compliance. This itself places them at a competitive disadvantage with the "drive-by-night" operators who operate with near impunity beyond the commercial zones which they have used to gain illegal entry into the intercity linehaul marketplace.

TTD AFFILIATES

The following labor organizations are members of and represented by the TTD:

Air Line Pilots Association
Amalgamated Transit Union
American Federation of State, County and Municipal Employees
American Federation of Teachers
American Train Dispatchers Department
Association of Flight Attendants
Brotherhood of Locomotive Engineers
Brotherhood of Maintenance of Way Employes
Brotherhood of Railroad Signalmen
Communications Workers of America
Hotel Employees and Restaurant Employees Union
International Association of Fire Fighters
International Association of Machinists and Aerospace Workers
International Brotherhood of Boilermakers, Blacksmiths, Forgers and Helpers
International Brotherhood of Electrical Workers
International Brotherhood of Firemen and Oilers
International Brotherhood of Teamsters
International Longshoremen's and Warehousemen's Union
Int' l Union, United Automobile, Aerospace and Agricultural Implement Workers of America
International Union of Operating Engineers
National Marine Engineers Beneficial Association
Retail, Wholesale and Department Store Union
Service Employees International Union
Sheet Metal Workers International Association
TransportationCommunications International Union
Transport Workers Union of America
United Brotherhood of Carpenters and Joiners of America
United Mine Workers of America
United Steelworkers of America
United Transportation Union

October 24, 1994

TRANSPORTATION TRADES DEPARTMENT, AFL-CIO

AMERICAN TRUCKING ASSOCIATIONS, INC.

THOMAS J. DONOHUE
PRESIDENT AND
CHIEF EXECUTIVE OFFICER

2200 MILL ROAD
ALEXANDRIA, VIRGINIA 22314-4677
(703) 838-1800

March 19, 1996

Mr. Charles A. Bowsher
Comptroller General
General Accounting Office
441 G Street, NW
Washington, DC 20548-0001

Dear Comptroller General Bowsher:

The American Trucking Associations staff was recently briefed about a February 1996 GAO report, *Commercial Trucking: Safety and Infrastructure Issues Under the North American Free Trade Agreement* (GAO/RCED-96-61). I want to let you know of my serious concerns about the report and offer a suggestion for further review by GAO.

This GAO report suffers from a number of serious flaws. Its analysis of North American truck safety is at best incomplete and therefore quite misleading. In many instances, the tone and balance of the report are disturbing. Even the title is misleading, as this is certainly not an account of "Safety and Infrastructure Issues Under the North American Free Trade Agreement," rather it is an account of the *status quo* prior to NAFTA. Overall, this report deals only superficially with the range of issues facing Congress on the future of North American truck transportation.

For example, the chart in the six-page body of the report contains an important factual error, one that is repeated again in the Appendix (see pages 4 and 20). It states that Mexico places "no limits" on hours of service. In fact, Mexico's basic labor law limits work to eight hours per day. Those restrictions apply to truck drivers. Factual errors of this sort fuel unjustified criticism of transportation under NAFTA.

Perhaps most disturbing, however, is the report's incomplete and misleading discussion of truck safety and international trucking. I'd like to elaborate just a bit.

(1) ***The report does not begin to deal adequately with what will actually happen under NAFTA, rather it focuses almost exclusively on the cross-border Mexican drayage trade within the U.S. border zone as it has existed for many decades.*** The report simply ignores a decisive fact taken for granted in the trucking industry: NAFTA's enhanced border access will require expensive compliance programs for Mexican carriers. Only the most capable and

sophisticated carriers are therefore likely to make use of NAFTA's enhanced access in the near future.

By failing to evaluate elementary facts about how the U.S. and Mexican industry plan to operate under NAFTA, the report unfairly implies that the entire Mexican motor carrier industry is lagging and will continue to lag in safety compliance. Moreover, the limited discussion of safety data related to the border zone drayage trade is presented in a form that sensationalizes the data rather than analyzes it.

A case in point. Based upon numbers in the report, we estimate that at least 165,000 trucks crossed the border during the three-week period analyzed. From the data provided, it appears that fewer than 1 percent of the vehicles that crossed were inspected. That means that roughly only 0.6 percent of the vehicles crossing the border were placed out of service.

More to the point, the sample of trucks inspected is not a representative or random sample of trucks currently crossing the border. Instead, experienced officers choose to inspect vehicles that appear to have problems. The fact that officers placed a large percentage of such vehicles out of service means that they were doing a good job of isolating problem trucks from the very substantial overall volume of traffic.

To be sure, trucks used in short-haul drayage operations across the border often *are* older and more prone to equipment failures than those used in long-haul transport on both sides of the border. That is one reason they are used in local, rather than long-haul trade. Indeed, one welcome aspect of NAFTA is that it is already focusing increased scrutiny and inspection resources on carriers operating in the border zone. Once the border is opened as provided by NAFTA, we expect gradually to see more long-haul firms operating into the border states.

(2) ***The report virtually ignores key elements of the massive government and private sector mobilization that had taken place to prepare for the border opening.*** The report states that "we evaluated the major implementation efforts associated with opening the U.S.-Mexican border to commercial trucking" (p. 1). Incredibly, the report is virtually silent about major state compliance preparations or the extensive industry safety training program sponsored by the states, the three NAFTA governments and the industry.

For example, the GAO reports prominently that Texas had 70 vehicle inspectors on duty on December 1 (p. 39). However, it says nothing about the 109 additional Texas motor carrier enforcement officials who were authorized for deployment after December 18. It says nothing about the additional vehicle inspection training provided by Texas for local police officers statewide. And it says nothing about the comprehensive safety training programs sponsored by the three governments with the industry's North American Transportation Alliance.

While it is critical of state enforcement capabilities, the report simply makes no serious effort to evaluate the state plans for NAFTA. For example, Thomas W. Ross, the California Highway Patrol's top NAFTA coordinator said in December, "we're ready to go when it's [NAFTA] implemented." Mike Cox, spokesman for Texas Governor George Bush, similarly told the press that "we're prepared to move forward when NAFTA goes into effect."

Trucking experts agree that the NAFTA border opening will not unleash an immediate, substantial tide of northbound truck traffic. In fact, the industry's phased-in use of the new access will give the states considerable time to adjust to the full demands of the new cross-border trade. Rather than cause a deterioration in truck safety, U.S. carriers believe that NAFTA's enhanced inspection regime will send a strong message to all foreign carriers: if you plan to operate in the U.S., you must meet *all* U.S. safety standards.

This flawed GAO report comes at a time when GAO's usual informed research and sober analysis are sorely needed by Congress, the public and the industry regarding NAFTA and motor carrier issues.

As you know, the expanded border access for trucking that was promised by NAFTA has now been delayed by our government. Precisely because the NAFTA border opening has become enmeshed in campaign-year politics, this GAO report may fuel greater misunderstanding about international trucking operations and related public policy issues.

Let me assure you that the American Trucking Associations and the industry we represent are committed to highway safety. We support increased inspections and have worked for additional funding for them. If a vehicle is unsafe, we believe that it should not be on our roads.

I would therefore encourage the GAO to devote additional resources to understanding the full range of issues related to commercial trucking under NAFTA. For example, it would be helpful to have GAO study the cross-border interline partnerships that link U.S. and Mexican firms. These are the long-haul carriers that will move the bulk of the increased NAFTA freight. Providing a more accurate and complete picture of international trucking operations and safety compliance would be welcome.

If the GAO does further work in this area, the American Trucking Associations will be happy to provide our full cooperation and assistance to your staff beginning at the outset of your study.

Sincerely,

Thomas J. Donohue
President & CEO

cc: Secretary Federico Peña
Administrator Rodney Slater
The Honorable Max Baucus
The Honorable Robert Byrd
The Honorable John Chafee
The Honorable Mark Hatfield
The Honorable Ernest Hollings
The Honorable Daniel Inouye
The Honorable Frank Lautenberg
The Honorable Trent Lott
The Honorable Larry Pressler
The Honorable John Warner
The Honorable Ronald Coleman
The Honorable Bob Livingston
The Honorable James Oberstar
The Honorable David Obey
The Honorable Thomas Petri
The Honorable Nick Rahall
The Honorable Bud Shuster
The Honorable Frank Wolf

Script

Final Edit

The True Cost of Winter Vegetables

Prepared by

Rafael F. Oller, M.F.A.

The Ninety Miles Film Company
1521 Alton Road, No. 113
Miami Beach, Florida 33139

TEL/FAX (305)864-7950
PAGER (305)955-2153

The True Cost of Winter Vegetables

Green Beans. Squash. Cucumbers. Eggplant. Bell peppers. Tomatoes.

From October to April, practically all Winter Vegetables grown in the U.S. come from one state: Florida, The Sunshine State, a State with a population of over **13 million**, shipping over **6 billion pounds** of fresh produce across the United States.

The Overall U.S. Winter Vegetable Market is valued at over **4 billion dollars**, and represents more than **50,000 U.S. jobs.**

It is a Market which until recently was dominated by U.S. farmers, providing for the American consumer, a price-stable, year-round supply of the safest and highest quality vegetables in the world.

A U.S. farming industry which is currently being forced toward extinction by the unguarded threat of winter vegetable imports from Mexico.

Just west of Mexico's Sierra Madre, encompassing an area larger than the State of California, Baja and the Sinaloa and Sonora Valleys export to the U.S over 2 1/2 billion pounds of the 6 Major Winter Vegetables, each year.

From October through April, over 110,000 truck loads of Mexican winter vegetables, cross the U.S. border, mostly through the port of Nogales.

Yet, due to the volume of shipments, only a fraction of the trailers can be closely inspected.

The U.S.D.A. checks the size and quality of imported tomatoes, but is not required to check the quality of any other winter vegetable.

F.D.A. tests for vegetable contamination are random. But, by the time the results return from the lab, those vegetables, identified as contaminated, will have already been shipped, sold, and consumed.

U.S. Customs also makes random spot checks.

Here a Customs agent checks for false walls in a cargo bay and the potential presence of contraband.

Yet, suprisingly, amidst the recent controversy regarding Mexican involvement in international drug trafficking, less than ten shipments of illegal narcotics were seized attempting to cross the border, this past year.

A majority of the winter vegetables shipments cross over 500 miles from deep within the Sinaloa Valley.

Culiacan, the capital of Sinaloa, boasts a population size roughly that of the State of Idaho.

Each year, during the last week of January, you will find the "Expo Agro, Sinaloa". A showcase prepared for growers from all over Mexico of the latest technological advances.

Foreign and domestic companies display their latest in farming equipment, fertilizers, and pesticides. Many of which end up in the storage sheds of growers throughout Mexico. Pesticides such as Malathion, Paraquat, Endosulfan, Methamidophos, Temik, Parathion.

A virtual grandstand of the latest and the greatest. Fortune 500 Companies such as New Holland, John Deere, Case, Texaco, Motorola, Monsanto.

All on display, for an entire weekend, offering Mexican farmers the opportunity to invest in greater productivity and crop yields.

In the 1980's, Mexico's share of the U.S. Winter Vegetable Market rarely exceeded 33%.

Yet, earlier this year, a leading Mexican University published a report stating that, last season, Mexico's market share of winter vegetables rose to 60%, with unprecedented numbers in five of the six major winter vegetables.

In the 1995/96 Season, Mexico's U.S. market share of Tomatoes alone rose to 68%. Bell peppers 64%, cucumbers and zucchini squash to 84%, and eggplant to 73%.

Of course, some of this market penetration could be explained by the recent, accelerated devaluation of the Mexican peso.

Prior to the implementation of NAFTA, in January 1994, the Mexican peso held at three pesos to the dollar. Before year's end, the peso had devaluated to half its value and now stands at close to eight pesos on the dollar, making the price, in U.S. dollars, of Mexican produce extremely attractive to U.S. buyers.

Fearing this potential market shift, the NAFTA agreement declared in a special provision, that certain winter vegetables were designated "sensitive crops" and established "snap-back" Tariff Rate Quotas.

Yet, suspecting unfair trade practices to be the true cause of this unprecedented, foreign market penetration, in April of 1996, Florida growers filed an antidumping action with the U.S. Department of Commerce alleging that Mexican producers were selling tomatoes in the U.S. market at prices below the cost of production.

And, in October of 1996, preliminary findings of the Commerce Department into the dumping of Mexican tomatoes found that Mexican tomatoes were being sold at lower than fair market prices, at times as much as 100 percent below the actual cost of production.

This prompted the negotiation of a suspension agreement between the Department of Commerce and the growers of Mexico to set the floor prices for Import shipments of tomatoes, a little over 5 dollars per box, which is much closer to the cost of U.S. produced tomatoes.

Yet, Mexican tomatoes are still cheaper to produce than those grown in the U.S., and it cannot all be blamed on the accelerated devaluation of the Mexican peso.

Other reasons, for the inequality in cost of vegetable production, might be found in the differences of each country's regulatory policies.

In the U.S., agriculture is heavily regulated by several agencies, while Mexican farmers remain relatively unsupervised.

Florida Farmer-owned housing comes under the jurisdiction of Florida's H.R.S.

In this Farmer-owned housing complex, in Palmetto, Florida, each adult field workers pays just **two dollars** per work day to live here.

On weekends its free, as it during time when there is no work.

During high season, that's about **one-hundred-and-twenty** dollars a month, per family, and that includes utilities.

For the most part, they are single family dwellings. Concrete floored, cinder block homes with running water and electricity and indoor bathrooms. Even a few essential furnishings are provided.

Some of the families have lived and worked here for over 15 years.

But in Mexico, lenient labor and housing requirements provide for the exploitation of relatively cheap labor.

Farmer provided housing is generally in the form of tar paper shacks. There are no toilet facilities, no electricity, no running water.

These children live with their family in a cramped, dirt-floor shack that doubles as a storage shed.

Field workers and their families are forced to use the surrounding irrigation ditches for drinking water, bathing, and washing clothes.

Often, less than a hundred yards away are the public toilets, which amount to little more than a sheltered hole in the ground.

Behind them, in the irrigation ditch, you can see floating raw sewage.

The average Mexican field worker earns from **twenty to thirty Mexican pesos** for an **eight hour day**. At current exchange rates, that translates to roughly **three U.S. dollars**. Compare that with a U.S. field worker who works the same amount of hours, on a piece incentive basis, and earns as much as **sixty dollars** in the day.

The U.S. Labor Department also restricts the minimum age of U.S. workers to sixteen. And you must be at least eighteen to work in a hazardous area.

Not so in Mexico. At times, you will find children barely old enough to go to school working in the packing sheds.

This boy selecting product-rejects from the conveyor belt and this girl channeling tomatoes for sorting are obviously way below the U.S. legal limit, and yet they are surrounded by potentially hazardous machinery.

On the average, the labor force in Mexico is relatively young in comparison to that of the U.S. But nowhere is this more endemic than in the fields.

It is current practice in the Mexican agricultural industry, to hire entire families to work the fields.

Children still too young to pick vegetables, sit in the shade of makeshift tents while their older brothers and sisters work side by side with their parents.

To earn a day's wages, children must pick as many bucket as the adults, and everyone must pick as many buckets as the one who has picked the highest quantity for that day, no matter how many hours it takes.

This girl, age seven, in the baseball cap, has been picking tomatoes since close to dawn.

The weight of the bucket is barely manageable, as she raises it to the gondola.

Recent editorials claim that it is a regional Mexican custom for children to work with their families.

But, one need not go too far, to see that this custom, more than anything is a custom fostered by the Mexican agricultural industry.

In the center of Culiacan, looking over the surrounding hedges of this day care center, one gets quite a different picture of the local customs.

Here the children are healthy and fully clothed, and given a provided a basic education.

In fact, this picture is much closer to that of the children of U.S. farm workers.

Children below the age of 16 are not permitted to work in the fields nor in the packing sheds, and school attendance is compulsory. A prime example of insightful legislation which offers quite a different prospect of the future.

But, the comparison gets worse.

In the U.S., the E.P.A. regulates all chemical pesticides, and strict guidelines must be met for their usage.

Remember those pesticides we saw at the "Expo Agro" and the Mexican grower sheds?

Five of them are designated for "restricted-use" pesticides.

Which means that to use them you must wear a flitered mask, your hands must be covered with rubber gloves, your feet must be properly covered, you must wear an impermeable suit.

And how are pesticides applied in Mexico?

Some farms use similar precautions.

But on this farm, a field worker mixes Paraquat, with his bare hands. An herbicide so acutely toxic, that as the label indicates, "It is fatal if swallowed, inhaled or absorbed through the skin. It can cause irrevesible eye damage. One swallow can kill!"

A serious matter, as the backpack sprayers are also not wearing any protective clothing.

U.S. Federal law requires pesticide application to be clearly posted. The area must also be clear of any unprotected field workers to prevent contamination from drift.

Not so in Mexico. Remember the field with the children? The field workers are taking a short lunch break, while pesticides are applied only a few yards away.

In the air, a dense cloud of the pesticide hover above their heads. Nearby, a mother nurses her infant.

In the U.S., the E.P.A. stipulates that no one is to enter a freshly sprayed field until the spray has dried, which could take hours.

Not so, in this field. Here the field workers, covering their mouths with their shirt tails, enter the field as the sprayer turns the corner to start on another row.

But worst of all, the pesticide the sprayers are applying is THIO VAC, an Endosulfan. A highly toxic pesticide with no specific antidote that attacks the central nervous system.

If it is swallowed you must pump the stomach.

If inhaled you must remove the victim to fresh air and apply respiration if required. Severe

Z

poisoning could result in death.

If it gets in the eyes, you must flush the eyes for 15 minutes with clean water.

But there is no water here, except in the water buffalos.

And that is the same water that comes from the irrigation ditch.

That is the same water we saw visible sewage floating in.

The same water used to wash vegetables before sorting and packing.

No doubt, in a very significant way, this lack of National regulations and standards, has allowed for Mexican growers to produce winter vegetables cheaper than those grown in the U.S.

Yet, better prices may result in greater risk. Since 1987, yearly outbreaks in the U.S. of food poisoning resulting the consumption of fresh produce have doubled, prompting the U.S. Centers for Disease Control and Prevention to more closely monitor all fresh produce.

Yet, as is common practice with fresh produce, its "country of origin" is rarely marked at the consumer level.

This also goes for canned and frozen vegetables. On these cans, nowhere does it state where the product you are about to eat is from.

Strange, when you consider that almost everything we use or wear is clearly labeled as to its country of origin.

The only State in the Union to have a "Country of Origin Labeling" law on its books is Florida.

A fortunate thing, as last year, during the "Cyclospora" outbreak on Guatemalan raspberries, Florida consumers were able to identify the product, avoid poisoning and purchase a safe alternative.

Yet, some fear, in the near future, there may not be any need for a "Country of Origin Labeling Law" for winter vegetables.

Since the implementation of NAFTA, the total economic loss in the production of fresh winter vegetables has been nearly **700 million** dollars, over **200** Florida farmers have gone out of business, and nearly **10,000** U.S. jobs have been lost.

Nowhere has this been more damaging than in the Florida tomato industry whose value as decreased from **607** million dollars in 1993, to **465** million dollars in 1994, to **387** million dollars in 1995, the lowest crop value in over a decade.

Yet, there is hope.

"The Imported Food Labeling Act" and the "International Child Labor Elimination Act".

"The Imported Food Labeling Act" seeks "to require origin of labeling of perishable commodities imported to the United States..."

The second bill: "The International Child Labor Elimination Act" seeks "to impose sanctions on countries that do no prohibit child labor."

Of course, the road of Mexico's economic development will be a long and difficult one.

But, with the passage of NAFTA, which has made Mexico a member of the largest trading block in the world, and through future effective U.S. legislation, such as those bills just mentioned, the spirit of free and fair trade can be preserved.

And in turn, provide the American consumer the cheapest, but safest and highest quality fresh produce in the world.

December 18, 1996

The Honorable William J. Clinton
President
The White House
1600 Pennsylvania Avenue, N.W.
Washington, D.C. 20500

Dear President Clinton:

One year ago today, the Administration announced a freeze on implementing the crossborder trucking provisions of NAFTA. Today, we still face a serious policy logjam. Your leadership is needed to find a fair and swift solution to this vital trade issue.

Mr. President, you courageously supported NAFTA in your first term because you knew it was good for America – good for the economy, good for business, and good for consumers. The NAFTA partnership *is* essential to our nation's future.

The freeze on crossborder trucking is not just a trucking issue. With over 85 percent of U.S.-Mexico trade moving by truck, NAFTA's overall success hinges on efficient crossborder trucking operations. Continued imposition of the freeze has strained our relations with Mexico, stymied resolution of other essential bilateral transportation issues, and denied the United States the benefits of expanded trade.

Like you, we are committed to moving traffic safely on our nation's highways and across our borders. However, the safety argument used to delay the border opening was based upon unsupported claims. Since the delay, state enforcement officials and the governors of the four Southern border states have said they are fully prepared to enforce the nation's safety regulations.

NAFTA promised to bring North American trade into the 21st century. You helped build the bridge that can bring us there. Now we are counting on your leadership to let us cross. Thank you for your help with this important matter.

Sincerely,

Thomas Donohue
President
American Trucking Associations

Edward Emmett
President
National Industrial Transportation League

The Honorable William J. Clinton
December 18, 1996
Page Two

Philip A. Vasquez
President
Commercial Vehicle Safety Alliance

Albert C. Zapanta
Executive Vice President
U.S.-Mexico Chamber of Commerce

José Niño
President & CEO
U.S. Hispanic Chamber of Commerce

Jerry J. Jasinowski
President
National Association of Manufacturers

Ambassador Everett E. Briggs
President
Council of the Americas

Andrew H. Card, Jr.
President & CEO
American Automobile Manufacturers Association

Gene S. Bergoffen
President & CEO
National Private Truck Council

Carlos Moore
Executive Vice President
American Textile Manufacturers Institute

Richard L. Lesher
President
U.S. Chamber of Commerce

Frank D. Kittredge
President
National Foreign Trade Council

The Honorable William J. Clinton
December 18, 1996
Page Three

The following individuals have also requested that their names be added as signatories to this letter:

Joel D. Anderson
Executive Vice President
California Trucking Association

Tracy Mullin
President
National Retail Federation

Richard Newpher
Executive Director
American Farm Bureau Federation

Vic J. Sheppard
Managing Director
New Mexico Motor Carriers Association

Terry Smalley
Executive Vice President
Arizona Motor Transport Association

William W. Webb
President
Texas Motor Transportation Association

**SIGNATORIES TO DECEMBER 18
LETTER TO PRESIDENT CLINTON**

Mr. Joel D. Anderson
Executive Vice President
California Trucking Association
11251 Beacon Boulevard
West Sacramento, CA 95691
(916) 373-3500

Mr. Gene S. Bergoffen
President
National Private Truck Council
66 Canal Center Plaza, Suite 600
Alexandria, VA 22314
(703) 683-1300

Ambassador Everett E. Briggs
President
Council of the Americas
1310 H Street, N.W., Suite 690
Washington, D.C. 20005
(202) 639-0724

Mr. Andrew H. Card, Jr.
President & CEO
American Automobile Manufacturers Association
1401 H Street, N.W., Suite 900
Washington, DC 20005
(202) 326-5500

Mr. Thomas Donohue
President & CEO
American Trucking Associations, Inc.
2200 Mill Road
Alexandria, VA 22314
(703) 838-1800

Mr. Edward M. Emmett
President
National Industrial Transportation League
17800 N. Moore Street, Suite 1900
Arlington, VA 22209
(703) 524-5011

Mr. Jerry J. Jasinowski
President
National Association of Manufacturers
1331 Pennsylvania Avenue, N.W., Suite 1500 North
Washington, D.C. 20004-1790
(202) 637-3000

Mr. Frank D. Kittredge
President
National Foreign Trade Council
1625 K Street, N.W., #1090
Washington, D.C. 20006
(202) 887-0278

Mr. Richard L. Lesher
President
U.S. Chamber of Commerce
1615 H Street, N.W.
Washington, D.C. 20062
(202) 659-6000

Mr. Carlos Moore
Executive Vice President
American Textile Manufacturers Institute
1801 K Street, N.W. Suite 900
Washington, D.C. 20006
(202) 628-0099

Ms. Tracy Mullin
President
National Retail Federation
325 7th Street, N.W.
Washington, D.C. 20004
(202) 783-7971

Mr. Richard Newpher
Executive Director
American Farm Bureau Federation
600 Maryland Avenue, SW, #400
Washington, D.C. 20006
(202) 484-3600

Mr. José Niño
President & CEO
U.S. Hispanic Chamber of Commerce
1030 15th Street, N.W., Suite 206
Washington, D.C. 20005
(202) 842-1212

Mr. Terry Smalley
Executive Vice President
Arizona Motor Transport Association
2111 West McDowell Road
Phoenix, AZ 85009
(602) 252-7559

Mr. Vic J. Sheppard
Managing Director
New Mexico Motor Carriers Association
4809 Jefferson Street, N.E.
Albuquerque, NM 87109
(505) 884-5575

Mr. Philip A. Vasquez
President
Commercial Vehicle Safety Alliance
5430 Grosvernor Lane, Suite 130
Bethesda, MD 20814
(301) 564-1623

Mr. William W. Webb
President
Texas Motor Transportation Association
P. O. Box 1669
Austin, TX 78701
(512) 478-2541

Mr. Albert C. Zapanta
Executive Vice President
U.S.-Mexico Chamber of Commerce
1726 M Street, N.W., Suite 704
Washington, D.C. 20036
(202) 296-5198

COMMERCIAL VEHICLE SAFETY ALLIANCE

An Association of State, Provincial and Federal Officials Responsible for the Administration and Enforcement of Motor Carrier Safety Laws in the United States, Canada and Mexico.

5430 GROSVENOR LANE • SUITE 130 • BETHESDA, MD 20814 • TEL.: (301) 564-1623 • FAX: (301) 564-0588

January 6, 1997

The Honorable William J. Clinton
President
The White House
1600 Pennsylvania Avenue, NW
Washington, DC 20500

Dear President Clinton:

On December 18, 1996, I co-signed a letter to you along with sixteen other trucking, automotive, and freight shipping industry groups, urging you to open the borders with Mexico and begin the implementation of NAFTA.

We mentioned in that letter that the state commercial vehicle enforcement and governors of the four Southern border states have said they are fully prepared to enforce this nation's safety regulations.

As President of the Commercial Vehicle Safety Alliance (CVSA), an association of Federal, State, and Provincial officials and inspection industry representatives responsible for enforcement of motor carrier safety laws in the United States, Canada, and Mexico, I want to reinforce the above statement and stress that from the safety perspective, we are prepared to deal with the cross-border traffic.

CVSA has played a key role in developing commercial vehicle safety enforcement procedures at the border crossings in the states of California, Arizona, New Mexico, and Texas. Through our International Affairs Committee, we have developed a comprehensive safety training for Mexican inspectors on the North American Vehicle Inspection Standard which has been used for some time both Canada and the United States. This training effort, along in with rapidly developing Intelligent Transportation System technologies that have already been tested at our border sites program, should ensure that Mexican commercial vehicles which crosses the border meet the U.S. safety standards.

And as you already know, the US. Department of Transportation has increased its commitment of resources and personnel to deal with increased border traffic.

In short, Mr. President, further delay serves no purpose. We will never know if we have taken all of the necessary steps until we actually put our present plans and procedures to work. If unforeseen problems develop, then we are prepared to take steps to deal with them.

In February of 1997, at the invitation of the Mexican transportation officials, CVSA's Executive Committee will be meeting in Mexico. NAFTA will be at the top of the meeting agenda. We are hoping that by then we can discuss implementation of the Treaty.

Mr. President, we stand ready to assist you in any way we can to make this happen.

Sincerely,

Phil Vasquez
President

CMA

CHEMICAL MANUFACTURERS ASSOCIATION

FREDERICK L. WEBBER
PRESIDENT AND CEO

December 18, 1996

The President
The White House
Washington, DC 20500

Dear Mr. President:

The ability to safely and efficiently transport chemicals throughout North America is of great significance to the chemical industry. One year ago, on December 18, 1995, the day that the cross-border trucking provisions of the North American Free Trade Agreement (NAFTA) were scheduled for implementation, the US government announced its decision to delay implementation of these provisions due to safety concerns. The purpose of writing to you now is to urge your Administration to immediately allow for cross-border trucking along the US-Mexican border.

The Chemical Manufacturers Association (CMA) is a nonprofit trade association whose member companies represent 90 percent of the productive capacity of basic industrial chemicals in the United States. Safety is of paramount importance to our member companies as shown by the membership's commitment to the Responsible Care® initiative. Responsible Care® requires CMA members to continuously improve their health, safety and environmental performance. CMA agrees that the methods used to implement the provisions of NAFTA must also protect the safety of the citizens and the environments of the US, Mexico and Canada. Yet we are also concerned that failure by any of the signatories to NAFTA to carry out the provisions prescribed by the agreement can harm the credibility of that party and may potentially jeopardize the entire agreement. Finally, further delay of these provisions will negatively impact the free flow of goods across the US-Mexican border, which will have serious economic consequences for the US chemical industry.

CMA, the Asociacion Nacional de la Industria Quimica, and the Canadian Chemical Producers' Association (respectively the chemical industry trade associations in Mexico and Canada) wrote to the Acting US Trade Representative in a letter dated May 28, 1996, regarding our concern about delaying implementation of these important NAFTA provisions. A copy is attached to this letter. CMA urges the US government to open the US-Mexican border for truck traffic, because we believe that operating authority should be granted to those Mexican truck operators that can demonstrate that they meet all required safety provisions necessary to operate in the United States.

For these reasons, CMA strongly encourages the US government to honor the provisions of NAFTA and to open the US-Mexican border for cross-border truck traffic. If you or your staff have questions or wish to discuss this letter, please contact Randy Speight, CMA, at (703) 741-5254.

Sincerely,

cc: The Honorable Charlene Barshefsky, Acting US Trade Representative
Jose Montemayor, Asociacion Nacional de la Industria Quimica
Richard Paton, Canadian Chemical Producers' Association

1300 WILSON BOULEVARD, ARLINGTON, VA 22209 • TELEPHONE 703-741-5100 • FAX 703-741-6086

Responsible Care®
A Public Commitment

12/19 '96 16:08 ID:ENG. DIV. ADM.

CATERPILLAR

Vice President

Caterpillar Inc.

Peoria, Illinois 61629

December 18, 1996

The Honorable William J. Clinton
President
The White House
1600 Pennsylvania Ave., N.W.
Washington, D.C. 20500

Dear Mr. President:

I respectfully ask that you continue to build on your bold leadership on the NAFTA agreement by opening the U.S.-Mexico border to trucking.

Caterpillar is a leading North American engine manufacturer, selling thousands of truck engines each year to truck manufacturers and individual customers in Mexico. The added logistical costs incurred by border regulations is passed along to all of our customers. If the current situation is prolonged, we anticipate a loss of business to our industry.

We understand and support the need to ensure safe trucking on U.S. highways. However, based on assurances from border state governors, we believe the active regulation of Mexican trucks will promote safety compliance.

Your leadership role in promoting the passage of NAFTA is appreciated. Early implementation of the border access provisions established by NAFTA is important to Caterpillar's long-term competitiveness and the efficiency of our freight movement.

Sincerely,

Gerald L. Shaheen

cc: The Honorable Federico Pena

CELADON GROUP INC.

One Celadon Drive
9503 E. 33rd St.
Indianapolis, IN 46236
Tel: (317) 972-7000
Fax: (317) 890-9414

December 11, 1996

The Honorable William J. Clinton
President
The White House
1600 Pennsylvania Ave., N.W.
Washington, D.C. 20500

Dear Mr. Clinton:

Celadon Trucking Services is, I believe, the leader in cross-border trucking between the U.S. and Mexico. We have approximately 2,000 employees and run about 1,500 tractors and 4,300 trailers. We are one of the largest transportation employers on the border, with facilities in Laredo, El Paso and elsewhere on the border. We move about 70,000 truckloads of freight annually between the U.S. and Mexico.

In March, 1996, I attended a meeting with other leaders in the transportation industry and Secretary Pena. I asked the Secretary about the intent of the Administration to adhere to the NAFTA Agreement allowing U.S. and Mexican tractors to cross the border to the adjacent state. He indicated that once the safety issues were resolved, the Administration intended to make the NAFTA regulation effective. (Incidentally, in 1973—when I was a thousand years younger than today—I was offered the position of Assistant Secretary for Transportation.)

Unless the U.S. government acts to open the border, congestion and interminable traffic delays will continue. Trade between the U.S. and Mexico is up over 25% from last year (Department of Commerce statistics). Because of the continued need to use three separate tractors to move freight between the U.S. and Mexico (a U.S. tractor, a crossing tractor, and a Mexican tractor), the delays have become even worse. The devaluation of the Peso has made Mexico an efficient producer of goods for the U.S. market...strangling the flow of cargo is counter-productive.

Your support to open the border is urgently requested. The DOT standards will be met, the adjoining state governors have already announced their support and the opening will be further enhanced by the trade between the U.S. and Mexico.

Sincerely,

Stephen Russell
Chairman and Chief Executive Officer

cc: Tom Donahue, ATA

caliber

Daniel J. Sullivan
Chairman, President and
Chief Executive Officer

Caliber System, Inc.
3560 W. Market Street
P.O. Box 5459
Akron, OH 44334-0459
Tel (330) 665-8800
Fax (330) 665-8803

December 17, 1996

The Honorable William J. Clinton
President
United States of America
1600 Pennsylvania Avenue, NW
Washington, DC 20500

Dear Mr. President:

My company, Caliber System, Inc., is a leading provider of value-added transportation, logistics and information related services. As Chairman, President and Chief Executive Officer of Caliber, I am requesting your support in opening the United States-Mexican border for cross-border trucking operations.

Transportation and logistics companies provide the crucial link between suppliers and manufacturers and their markets, not only in this country but around the world. Your administration recognized the need for opening our borders to trade with Mexico and, through your personal and forceful leadership, was instrumental in gaining approval of NAFTA. The transportation industry, and its partners in state and local governments in the United States and Mexico, are prepared now to initiate operations in the United States and the Mexican border states.

I respectfully submit that continued delay of implementation not only retards the beneficial impact of NAFTA, but also delays the resolution of other trucking issues with Mexico. Our customers have asked us to serve their markets as efficiently and effectively as possible. With your support for immediate trucking operations between the United States and Mexican border states, our industry will be in a better position to meet the needs of those customers.

Thank you for your consideration of my comments.

Sincerely,

Daniel J. Sullivan

Frederick W. Smith
Chairman of the Board and Chief Executive Officer

Federal Express Corporation
2005 Corporate Avenue
Memphis, TN 38132

US Mail: PO Box 727
Memphis, TN 38194-1841

Telephone 901 395-3377
Fax 901 398-1111

FedEx.
Federal Express

December 17, 1996

The Honorable William J. Clinton
President
The White House
1600 Pennsylvania Avenue, NW
Washington, DC 20500

Dear Mr. President:

Federal Express fully supports an immediate opening of the U.S.-Mexico border for crossborder transportation services into the U.S. and Mexico border states.

As part of our integrated express network, Federal Express is prepared to institute crossborder services between the U.S. and Mexico as soon as your Administration opens the border. We suggest that permitting services like those of Federal Express will enure to the economic benefit of both nations.

We urge your immediate consideration of this extremely important issue.

Sincerely,

FWS:clh.40702.1

cc: The Honorable Frederico Peña

VIA FEDEX OVERNIGHT LETTER

SCHNEIDER. NATIONAL

Customer Service/Corporate Business Center

December 16, 1996

The Honorable William J. Clinton
President
The White House
1600 Pennsylvania Avenue, N.W.
Washington, D.C. 20500

Dear Mr. President:

I am writing to request your personal involvement in opening the United States-Mexico border to trucking.

As you know, this opening was originally scheduled to occur Dec. 18 of last year, but was unilaterally postponed by the United States. Since then, no new opening date has been announced. Whatever reason or merit there may have been in the original decision to delay the border opening, now is the time to put this matter back on track.

The border opening is not just an issue for trucking companies. It affects all of us. On a direct basis, it has an impact on our ability to get our goods from suppliers and to their customers. The system in place today is a mess, and greatly affects the cost of our services and thus our customer's products. While opening the border will not, in and of itself, solve all the problems related to international movements, it is the necessary first step towards reform.

This issue also affects us on an indirect basis. As you know, trade matters seldom exist in a vacuum. Disputes in one area tend to have repercussions in others. Indeed, this particular issue seems to have become the lightening rod for NAFTA opponents on both sides of the border. American opponents see this delay as a means of thwarting all NAFTA related efforts at integration. Mexican opponents similarly use it as a means to justify all resistance to efforts to open and reform their economy. Opening the border will demonstrate once and for all that NAFTA is a fact of life and here to stay.

This is important to my company because NAFTA benefits us. Schneider National employs more than 13,000 associates in the United States, and these jobs are dependent upon trade of one sort or another. Our people either move goods directly, or figure out how it is to be done. We are not afraid of greater competition. In fact, we welcome it, because we believe we have the skills, ability and desire to thrive in an open, honest environment.

Mr. President, your leadership helped NAFTA come into being in the first place. We again need your leadership to get implementation back on course. On behalf of my company, I am asking for your support in making that happen.

Very truly yours,

Donald J. Schneider,
President

P.O. Box 2545 Green Bay, Wisconsin 54306 414-592-2000

NP 498-0006 2/96

ROADWAY Express Inc.

1077 GORGE BOULEVARD • P.O. BOX 471 • AKRON, OH 44309-0471

MICHAEL W. WICKHAM
PRESIDENT & CEO

(330) 384-1717 • FAX: (330) 258-6082
E-MAIL ADDRESS: mwickham@roadway.com
www.roadway.com

December 12, 1996

The Honorable William J. Clinton
President
The White House
1600 Pennsylvania Avenue, N.W.
Washington, DC 20500

Dear President Clinton:

On behalf of the 26,000 Roadway Express, Inc., employees, I congratulate you for your courageous leadership in obtaining approval of NAFTA. The unprecedented increase in U.S./Mexico trade has been a direct result of your leadership. Both countries have benefited from this agreement.

We at Roadway Express have expended considerable effort and investment to be a major service provider in the safe and efficient transportation of goods and materials between Mexico, Canada, and the U.S. We have formed relationships with Mexican trucking companies and actively support the Commercial Vehicle Safety Alliance (CVSA) to ensure the safety of all trucks crossing the border in both directions. Roadway Express is ready to provide safe and efficient transportation services between the U.S. and Mexico.

I urge you to consider an immediate opening of the U.S./Mexico border for cross-border trucking between the U.S. and Mexican border states. Opening the border now will provide for the continued implementation of NAFTA and the efficient movement of goods across our borders.

We at Roadway Express look forward to working with your administration on the implementation of NAFTA and many other important issues facing our nation and industry.

Please accept my best wishes for a happy holiday and a successful 1997!

Sincerely,

M Wickham

cc: Honorable Federico Pena - Sec. U.S. DOT
Honorable Thomas C. Sawyer - U.S. House of Representatives

TMTA
Texas Motor Transportation Association
700 East 11th Street • Austin, Texas 78701
Phone: (512) 478-2541 • Fax: (512) 474-6494

December 16, 1996

The Honorable William J. Clinton
President
The White House
1600 Pennsylvania Avenue, N.W.
Washington, D.C. 20500

Dear President Clinton:

It has been one year since the Administration announced a freeze on implementing the crossborder trucking provisions of the North American Free Trade Agreement. As of this writing, we still have no solution to this serious issue. Even worse, we appear to have no solution in sight for businesses trying to operate within the framework of NAFTA.

Your past support of NAFTA is appreciated. However, the benefits that will result from this agreement cannot be fully realized until the border is open and trade is allowed to occur in the tradition of the U.S. free market system.

Many manufacturing companies and transportation companies spent millions of dollars to develop resources and facilities to comply with, and take full advantage of, the NAFTA provisions. People were hired, buildings were built, and lives were impacted in order to meet the December 18, 1995 implementation date. The freeze negatively impacted those companies who had followed your lead in supporting NAFTA.

It is very difficult to plan for future business activities with no firm commitment on the Administration's part on when the border will open in accordance with the ratified NAFTA agreement. I know part of your platform is for growth in the U.S. economy and for businesses to flourish, thereby creating new jobs for the citizens of our great country. The current situation is stifling business and costing motor carriers, manufacturers, and many others millions of dollars each month this freeze remains in place.

Our state agencies, the same people who have been given the authority to enforce NAFTA provisions, tell us they are ready for the border to open. Businesses tell us they are ready for the border to open. Companies in Mexico tell us they are ready for the border to open. On behalf of the more than 28,000 companies operating commercial vehicles in the state of Texas, I urge you to release the freeze and allow NAFTA to operate as it was designed. This is a vital issue to our state and its citizens.

Thank you for your consideration.

Sincerely,

Bill Webb

Bill Webb
President

DEC. 16 '96

NEW MEXICO MOTOR CARRIERS' ASSOCIATION, INC.
4809 JEFFERSON NE • ALBUQUERQUE, NM 87109-2102 • (505) 884-5575 FAX 884-3661

December 16, 1996

The Honorable William J. Clinton
President
The White House
1600 Pennsylvania Ave. NW
Washington, DC 20500

Dear Mr. President:

I would like to take this opportunity to urge you to use your influence to effect an immediate opening of the U.S. - Mexico border for cross border trucking operations into the U.S. and Mexico border states. The decision to delay the December 18, 1995 opening has caused the trucking industry in New Mexico to lose opportunities and revenue, while undermining the U.S. governments commitment to NAFTA and expanded trade to Mexico.

Opening of the border would lead to greater efficiencies, savings in costs and time and would greatly facilitate the flow of commerce across our mutual border. This delay has made progress on other bilateral trucking issues impossible.

The vast majority of freight with Mexico is moved by trucks and the state of New Mexico had anticipated unprecedented growth in this arena, sadly that has failed to materialize.

Safety was the primary issue in not initiating the opening and yet safety enforcement officials and the four Southern border state governors have said they are fully prepared to enforce the nation's safety regulations. The administration hasn't yet even established the conditions that would allow for implementation for the border access provisions established under NAFTA.

As a result of the freeze on cross border trucking, service contracts were broken and equipment orders were canceled. The current inefficient and congested border crossing process for freight movements has been perpetuated.

More importantly, this act has undermined America's international credibility and our prospects for long-term economic growth. Make no mistake, Mr. President, the Pacific rim countries are ready to fill the economic gap that the U.S. actions have created in Mexico.

Once again, I urge you to effect the immediate opening of the U.S. - Mexican border as promised.

Sincerely,

Victor J. Sheppard
Managing Director

VJS/amm

cc: Secretary Pena, U.S. Dept of Transportation

Strength in Unity

SLS INC.
Sears Logistics Services, Inc.
3333 Beverly Road
Hoffman Estates, IL 60179
Phone: 847-645-5100

December 18, 1996

The Honorable William J. Clinton
President
The White House
1600 Pennsylvania Avenue, N.W.
Washington, D.C. 20500

Dear Mr. President:

I am writing to request your personal involvement in opening the United States-Mexico border to trucking.

As you know, this opening was originally scheduled to occur Dec. 18 of last year, but was unilaterally postponed by the United States. Since then, no new opening date has been announced. Whatever reason or merit there may have been in the original decision to delay the border opening, now is the time to put this matter back on track.

The border opening is not just an issue for trucking companies. It affects all of us. On a direct basis, it has an impact on our ability to get our goods from our suppliers. The system in place today is a mess. While opening the border will not, in and of itself, solve all the problems related to international movements, it is the necessary first step towards reform.

This issue also effects us on an indirect basis. As you know, trade matters seldom exist in a vacuum. Disputes in one area tend to have repercussions in others. Indeed, this particular issue seem to have become the lightening rod for NAFTA opponents on both sides of the border. American opponents see this delay as a means of thwarting all NAFTA related efforts at integration. Mexican opponents similarly use it as means to justify all resistance to efforts to open and reform their economy. Opening the border will demonstrate once and for all that NAFTA is a fact of life and here to stay.

This is important to SLS because NAFTA facilitates our ability to operate more cost effectively. Open borders can only help the retail and logistics industry.

Mr. President, your leadership helped NAFTA come into being in the first place. We again need your leadership to get implementation back on course. On behalf of this company, I am asking for your support in making that happen.

Sincerely,

SEARS LOGISTICS SERVICES, INC.

Roger Will

Roger Will
Vice President Transportation

RW:jn

EXECUTIVE OFFICE OF THE PRESIDENT
OFFICE OF THE UNITED STATES TRADE REPRESENTATIVE
WASHINGTON, D.C. 20508

HEARING OF THE INTERNATIONAL ECONOMIC POLICY AND TRADE SUBCOMMITTEE OF THE HOUSE INTERNATIONAL RELATIONS COMMITTEE REGARDING NAFTA REPORT CARD MARCH 5, 1997

Supplementary responses from Ambassador Ira Shapiro, Senior Counsel and Negotiator, Office of the U.S. Trade Representative

Question

Rep. Clement: Yes, I have one more question. Let me ask the one more question, and then you can respond to both. Fourteen months ago, the Administration delayed implementation of [the] NAFTA provisions that would allow Mexican motor carriers to operate anywhere in California, New Mexico, Arizona, and Texas. It is my understanding that the safety and security concerns that led to this decision have not been resolved, and remain just as serious. Is the Administration considering removing current restrictions?

Answer

The Administration remains committed to NAFTA and its promise of economic prosperity for North America. We fully intend to honor our NAFTA obligation to permit Mexican motor carriers to operate in the United States. To that end, we have identified a number of steps that the United States and Mexico can take together that will benefit motor carriers and their customers while enhancing public safety and security in both countries. For example, the Department of Transportation is assisting Mexico in the training of truck inspectors and in the development of a driver information exchange system that is compatible with the U.S. driver database. Also, we continue to make significant progress towards making the countries' safety standards more compatible.

In negotiations over the past 15 months, the United States, Canada, and Mexico have agreed on a strategy to assure that all motor carriers are in compliance with their safety obligations prior to beginning cross-border operations. The countries have agreed on critical safety areas that will be reviewed and approved by each country's authorities before a carrier can begin cross-border operations, including: (1) safety management systems; (2) driver qualifications; (3) hours of service compliance; (4) drug and alcohol testing; (5) condition of vehicle; (6) accident monitoring programs; and (7) compliance with regulations governing the transportation of hazardous materials. U.S. and Mexican transportation officials are currently discussing a timetable for Mexico to implement specific elements of its compliance and enforcement program. We expect to resolve outstanding issues in the near future in order to be able to implement the land transportation access provisions without compromising public safety.

Question

Rep. Sherman: A related question goes back to the issues of truck safety that Bob brought up. And that is, I represent a border state. I'm particularly concerned that trucks that are too large and too old, driven by drivers that have no particularly effective regulation are going to be causing automobile accidents. And there's no effective way to make sure that there's proper insurance. Now, monetary compensation doesn't really compensate for a tragedy like that. But is there any provision in NAFTA that would have the U.S. Government step in and pay someone who was terribly mangled by a poorly trained and poorly licensed driver from Mexico on our streets driving there pursuant to NAFTA?

Answer

All foreign motor carriers operating in the United States must comply with the same federal and state regulations that apply to U.S. carriers. These include safety regulations, weights and dimensions requirements, insurance requirements, tariff requirements where applicable, and all taxes and fees. Foreign carriers are also subject to U.S. immigration, customs, and labor laws. Let me address the specific points that you have raised.

- There are no provisions in the NAFTA that would require the U.S. Government to pay damages to the victims of accidents caused by Mexican drivers operating in the United States. The same laws and procedures that apply to the payment of compensation in other accidents occurring on U.S. soil would apply to Mexican driver-related accidents.

- Mexican motor carriers operating in the United States must meet the same financial responsibility requirements as U.S. motor carriers. Currently, Mexican motor carriers that operate within the border commercial zones may obtain trip insurance. Once the NAFTA is implemented, Mexican motor carriers operating beyond the commercial zones must show proof of continuous insurance coverage. Motor carriers can meet these requirements by filing certificates of insurance or other securities or agreements in the amounts prescribed. The companies are required to obtain insurance from a company licensed to do business in at least one state in the United States. Insurance companies are required to notify DOT immediately if a motor carrier's insurance lapses. In that event, the motor carrier is prohibited from operating. Truckers' insurance documents are examined during routine inspections.

- Mexican drivers engaged in cross-border transportation must have a valid commercial drivers license issued by Mexico's Secretariat of Communications and Transportation. In November 1991, after more than two years of work by U.S. and Mexican transportation officials, the United States and Mexico signed a Memorandum of Understanding recognizing the reciprocity of each other's licensing standards. The Department of Transportation has determined that commercial drivers licenses issued by the Government of Mexico in conformity with its national safety standards are in accordance with the U.S. standard set forth in 49 CFR Part 383. Mexico also has adopted U.S.-compatible age and language requirements for commercial drivers involved in cross-border operations. In addition, the NAFTA countries are developing a North American logbook, modeled after the U.S. and Canadian logbooks, to track drivers' hours of service and rest periods. Thus, Mexican drivers operating in the United States must possess qualifications similar to those of U.S. drivers.

The three NAFTA countries, as members of the Commercial Vehicle Safety Alliance, have adopted a basic commercial vehicle safety standard as the minimum level of mechanical fitness to be sustained by all commercial motor vehicles operating in international commerce. The Department of Transportation is working with Mexican officials to train and deploy Mexican inspectors throughout the country to ensure that northbound trucks are checked before they reached the U.S. border. On the U.S. side, enforcement efforts have been strengthened through additional funding under the Motor Carrier Safety Assistance Program for the border states' safety compliance activities. In addition, the states have committed their own resources to enforce motor carrier safety and operating requirements as NAFTA is implemented. For example, the State of California has made substantial investments in infrastructure and personnel, as evidenced in the state-of-the-art inspection facilities installed at California's busiest border crossings at Otay Mesa and Calexico.

April 9, 1997

REPORT CARD ON NAFTA

March 26, 1997

The Subcommittee on International Economic Policy and Trade of the House Committee on International Relations

National Association of Independent Insurers
2600 River Road, Des Plaines, IL 60018-3286

THE SUBCOMMITTEE ON INTERNATIONAL ECONOMIC POLICY AND TRADE
OF THE
HOUSE COMMITTEE ON INTERNATIONAL RELATIONS

Statement by
Gerald W. Bell
Director — Commercial & Property Lines

REPORT CARD ON NAFTA

The National Association of Independent Insurers (NAII) is heartened by the fact that you convened an open hearing before your subcommittee on March 5th for the purpose of "hearing a report card on the NAFTA" as commented in your opening statement. NAII supports the Preamble and Objectives (Part One, Chapter One, Article 102) of the NAFTA. Nonetheless, our Association is greatly concerned that the current reality falls alarmingly short of these stated ideals...short enough in fact to conclude that it would be irresponsible for the Clinton Administration to lift the moratorium at this time. The threats to life safety, the environment, and the infrastructure are simply too great.

The National Association of Independent Insurers, better known as the NAII, is a large, fast growing major property insurance trade association representing more than 560 member insurance companies. The Association's members produce and service nearly 26% of all the property and casualty insurance business in the nation. More specifically, NAII members insure about one-third (33%) of all the large trucks in the United States.

The NAFTA requires the parties to work together to *enhance the level* of safety and of protection of human, animal and plant life and health, the environment and consumers (Article 906.1). Compatibility of standards is to be achieved to the greatest extent possible, *without reducing the level of safety* (Article 906.2.).

Parties to the Land Transportation Standards Subcommittee and to its Technical Advisory Groups have worked diligently to negotiate agreements and to achieve compatibility on many issues. That is laudable. However, the reality, Madam Chairwoman, is that the *level* of safety has not been significantly enhanced since the NAFTA went into effect three years ago.

Let's look at some facts:

- Over 11,000 trucks enter the United States border zone each day. They cross at any of 28 highway points of entry. More than 4,000 of those trucks enter at Laredo, Texas, the busiest point. Concern about the potential environmental impact of a hazardous material spill from incoming Mexican trucks is so great in Laredo, Texas, that the local television stations run frequent public service videos warning residents about the threat.

- The United States Department of Transportation has once again entered into agreement with Mexican officials to provide training for Mexican enforcement personnel regarding U.S. motor carrier standards for vehicles and operators. A February 1996 General Accounting Office report advises that since 1993 U.S. officials trained 285 Mexican personnel to inspect trucks. Those personnel were to have become the trainers in Mexico, but most have left the program according to Mexican officials. Why should we believe that this new effort will bear a different result?

- The Governors of the four U.S. border states have widely proclaimed that their states are ready for the moratorium to be lifted and that unsafe Mexican trucks will be weeded out, but we are not convinced that effective systems are in place yet to assure safety. None of the border states appear to have the requisite number of enforcement personnel to assure that even the majority of unsafe Mexican trucks will be weeded out.

    - Texas Attorney General Dan Morales reported in early 1996 that of the 5,000 commercial vehicles entering Texas each day that only about 150 (3%) are stopped and inspected by Texas

Department of Public Safety troopers.

- Karen Hughes, a spokesperson for the Governor, is quoted in the November 30, 1996 Fort Worth Star Telegram as saying, "The Texas Department of Public Safety *is fully prepared* to make sure that *all* the trucks meet safety standards." Ms Hughes remark seems inconsistent with a comment by the Governor on January 28th that 109 additional troopers will be added to the Public Safety Department in order to enforce safety and weight laws.

- Even Mexican business community spokespersons are having second thoughts about the NAFTA.

  - On February 3rd, Alfredo Cardenas, Vice President of Mexico's National Chamber of Cargo Transport was quoted by Reuter News Service as saying, "I believe it will be negative to open the border because the economic conditions between the countries are very different."

  - The news service also quoted Cardenas, speaking in his capacity as director of Mexico's fourth-largest trucking company, as saying, "It will damage Mexicans because no Mexican can compete with the Americans. It should wait until our economy recovers in three to five years more."

  - Bernardo Lijtzain Bimstein, President of the Mexican national trucking association known as CANACAR, was quoted by the Journal of Commerce as saying, "We are not in a position to compete with the Americans. The longer the opening is put off, the more time we have to prepare."

- The true economic impact of the NAFTA must take into consideration the costs expended by the federal and state governments to enforce vehicle and driver safety standards.

  - The state of California constructed new Highway Patrol Inspection facilities at Otay Mesa and at Calexico at a cost of

$30 million.

- Texas is adding 109 State Troopers at a cost estimated to exceed $4 million.

- The United States Customs Service has installed the world's largest (and presumably among the most expensive) X-ray machines at its Otay Mesa facility, capable of X-raying an entire 53 foot semi-trailer at one time.

- Texas has constructed a new roadside enforcement facility at El Paso at an estimated cost of $700 thousand.

- New Mexico has constructed a new inspection facility at Anthony at an approximate cost of $9 million.

- The NAFTA provides that each party will comply with the laws of its tri-lateral trading partners. These include laws relating to commercial motor vehicle, drivers, and the environment. The reality however is that Mexican trucks and their operators enter the U.S. out of compliance with applicable statutes and regulations, with relative impunity. While the training and proficiency of U.S. and state enforcement personnel is high they are dangerously understaffed. Only a minuscule number of Mexican trucks can be inspected each day...too small a percentage to serve as a deterrent to those who see the chance of their getting caught to be minimal.

  - The maximum legal weight limit for a truck engaged in interstate commerce is 80,000 pounds. Rob Harrison, associate director of the transport research center at the University of Texas is quoted in the January 17th Journal of Commerce as saying, "Some loads entering the border zone approach 150,000 pounds." It has long been reported that Mexican officials have not aggressively enforced weight limits. Roadside scales are virtually nonexistent.

  - Mexican environmental law provides for a maximum sulfur content in diesel fuel. The national oil company, Pemex, produces diesel containing 50% more sulfur content than permitted by Mexican law (300 percent more than permitted by U.S. standards). Pemex is the sole source of diesel fuel in Mexico. Trucks incoming from Mexico will be belching their hazardous fumes into the U.S. environment, thus exacerbating existing acid rain, respiratory and other health concerns.

- The Otay Mesa port of entry is the busiest in California. From the seven month period December 1, 1995 through June 30, 1996, 250,613 Mexican trucks passed through the California Highway Patrol Inspection Facility. All vehicles passed over the scales. However, only 5,744 trucks (2.3%) were physically inspected. Of these 5,744 inspections 3,567 (62%) resulted in citations for one or more violations. 1,412 (25%) of the inspected vehicles were placed "out-of-service on the spot.

- At the Calexico, California port of entry the percentage of inspected commercial vehicles placed out-of-service is 30% according to Vince Calderon, a California Highway Patrol inspection officer.

NAII appreciates the opportunity to submit these brief comments for the hearing record. As to the report card:

'A' — for good intentions, desires, determinations, resolutions, agreements, alliances, accords, assurances, and promises.

'F' — for significant results that currently reduce the triple threats...life safety, environment, infrastructure.

ISBN 0-16-056023-3
90000
9 780160 560231

APEX
TP
9780160560231
76901945 – 82